PicTrix™ Vol.1

THE ORIGINAL BOOK OF PICTURE TRICKS

PicTrix™ Vol 1
The Original Book of Picture Tricks
Copyright 1991 by PicTrix™ Publishing. All rights reserved.
Printed in the United States of America.
For information write PicTrix™ Publishing
3131 SW Martin Downs Blvd. Suite 345
Palm City, Florida 34990

PicTrix is a Trademark of Paul J. Gruen

ISBN: 0-9630521-0-1

PicTrix™ Picture Puzzle Instructions

- The clue in the upper left hand corner refers to the word that you are trying to find.

- Each picture on the page contains one correct "sound" that represents a part of the word.

- When the "sounds" are put together they create the word.

- The pictures are "read" from left to right and the "sounds" are always in that order.

1

Centrifugal Toy

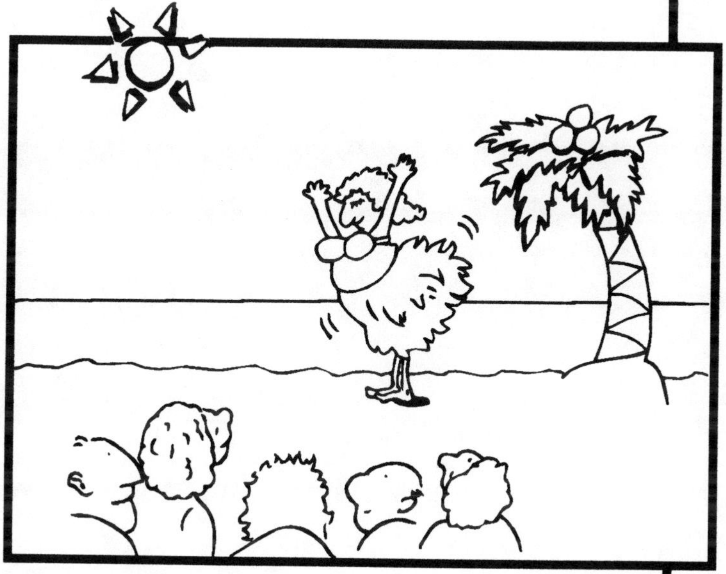

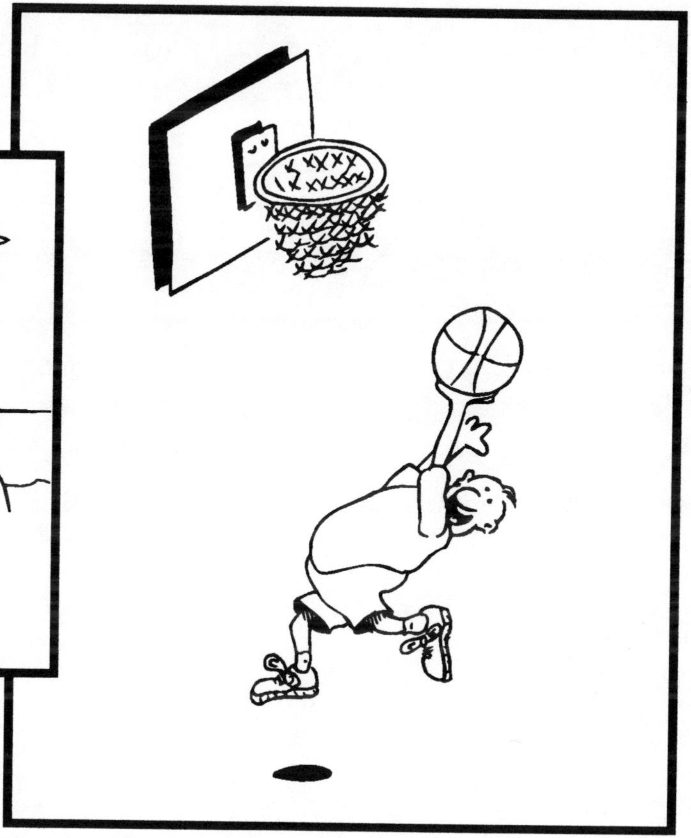

ANSWER ON BACK

HOOLA HOOP

2

Used to gain leverage

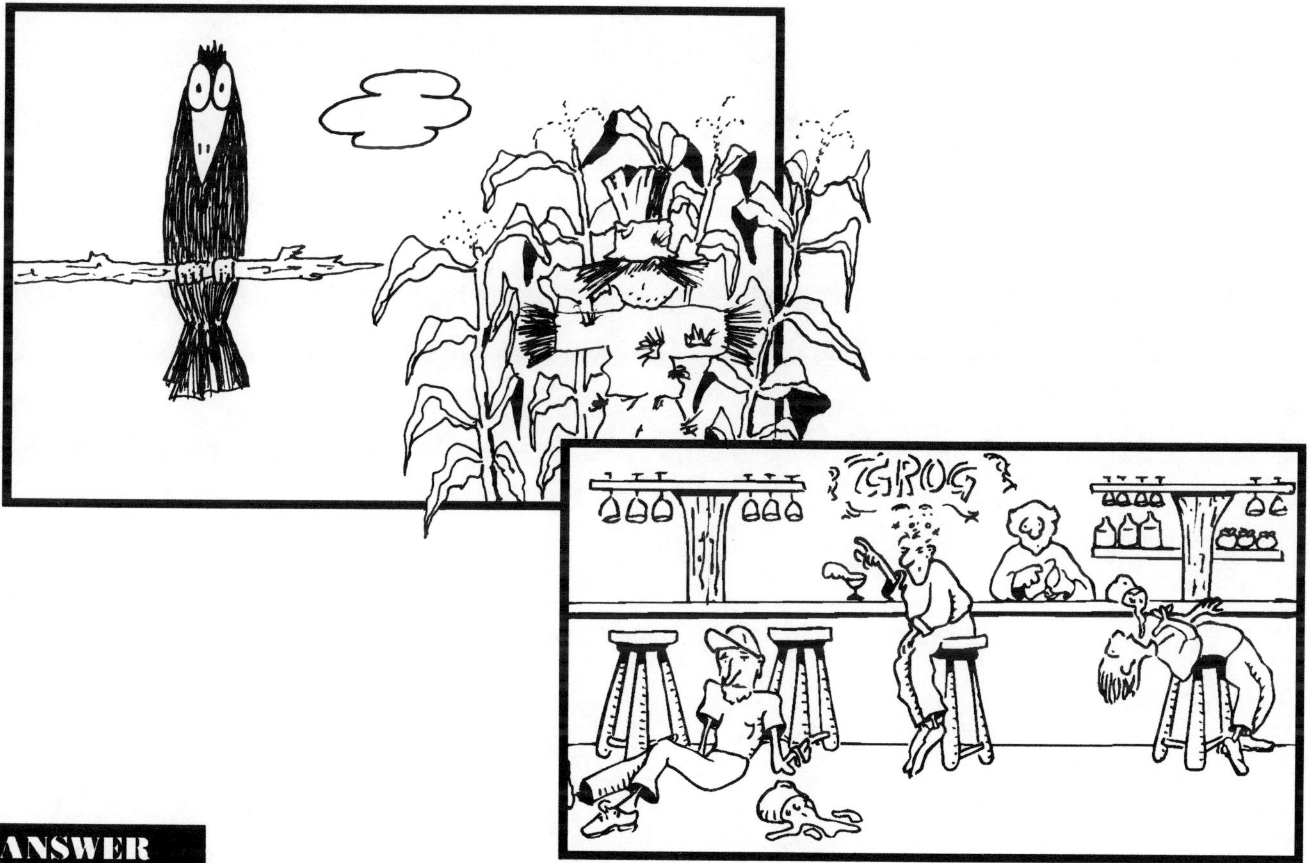
GROG

ANSWER ON BACK

CROWBAR

Statement at the front door

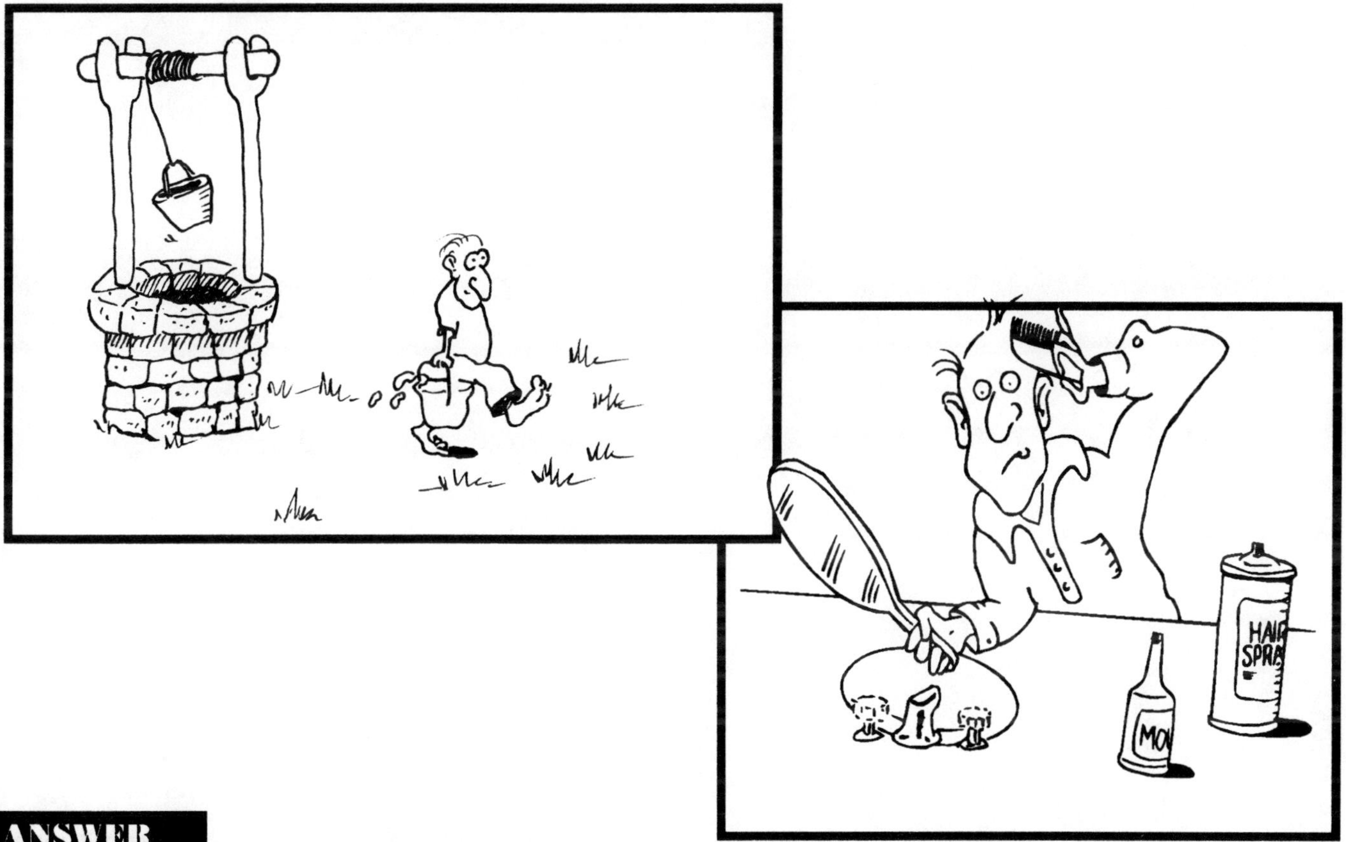
HAIR
SPRA
MO

ANSWER ON BACK

WELCOME

4

Adjective for when adults act childish

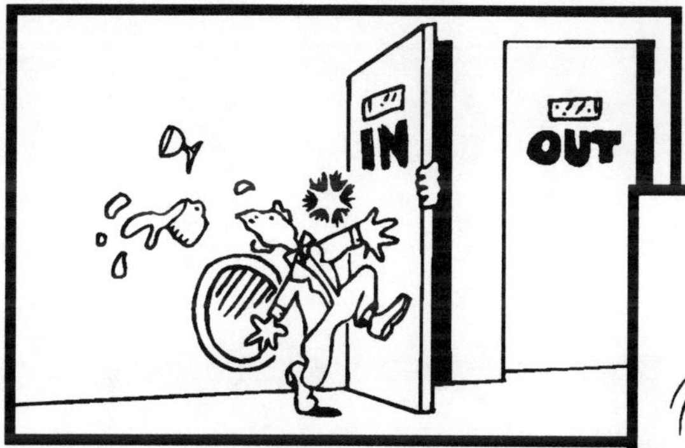
IN
OUT

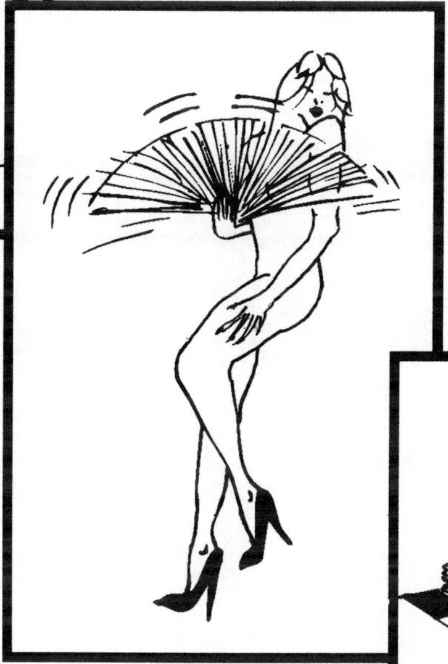

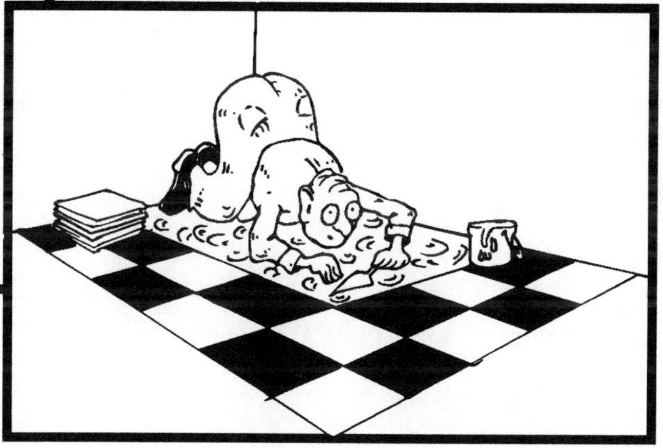

ANSWER ON BACK

INFANTILE

5

A bonus for brains or sports expertise

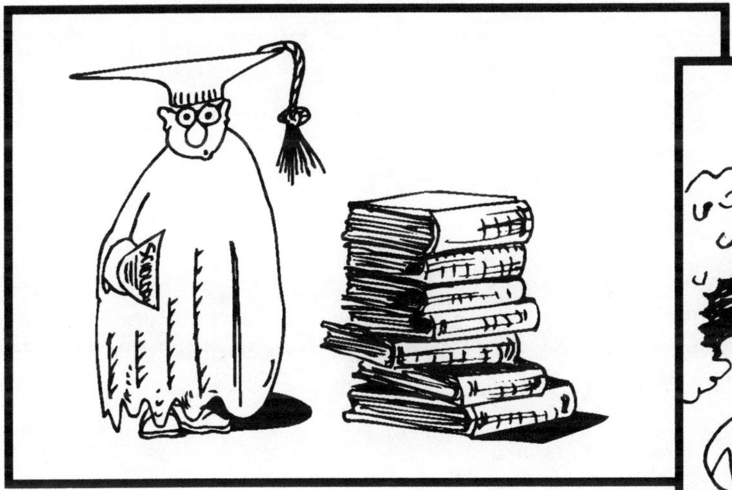

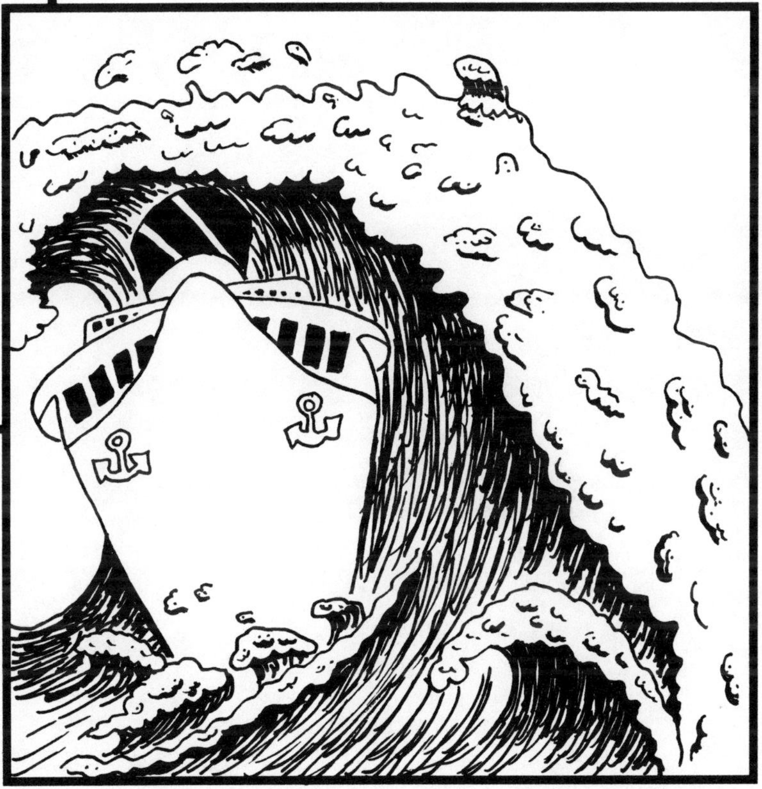

ANSWER ON BACK

SCHOLORSHIP

6

A big time movie studio

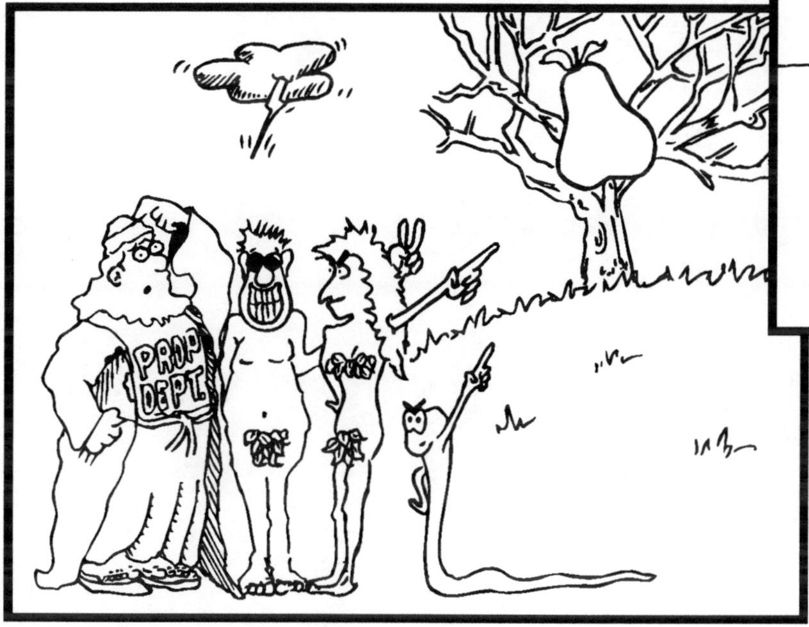
PROP DEPT.

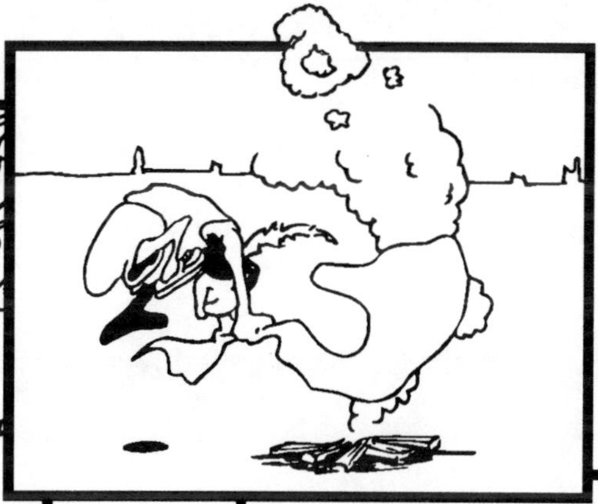

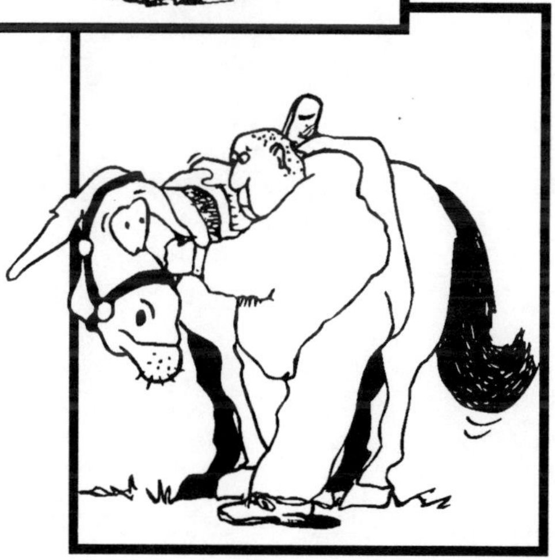

ANSWER ON BACK

PARAMOUNT

7

4th of July Ritual

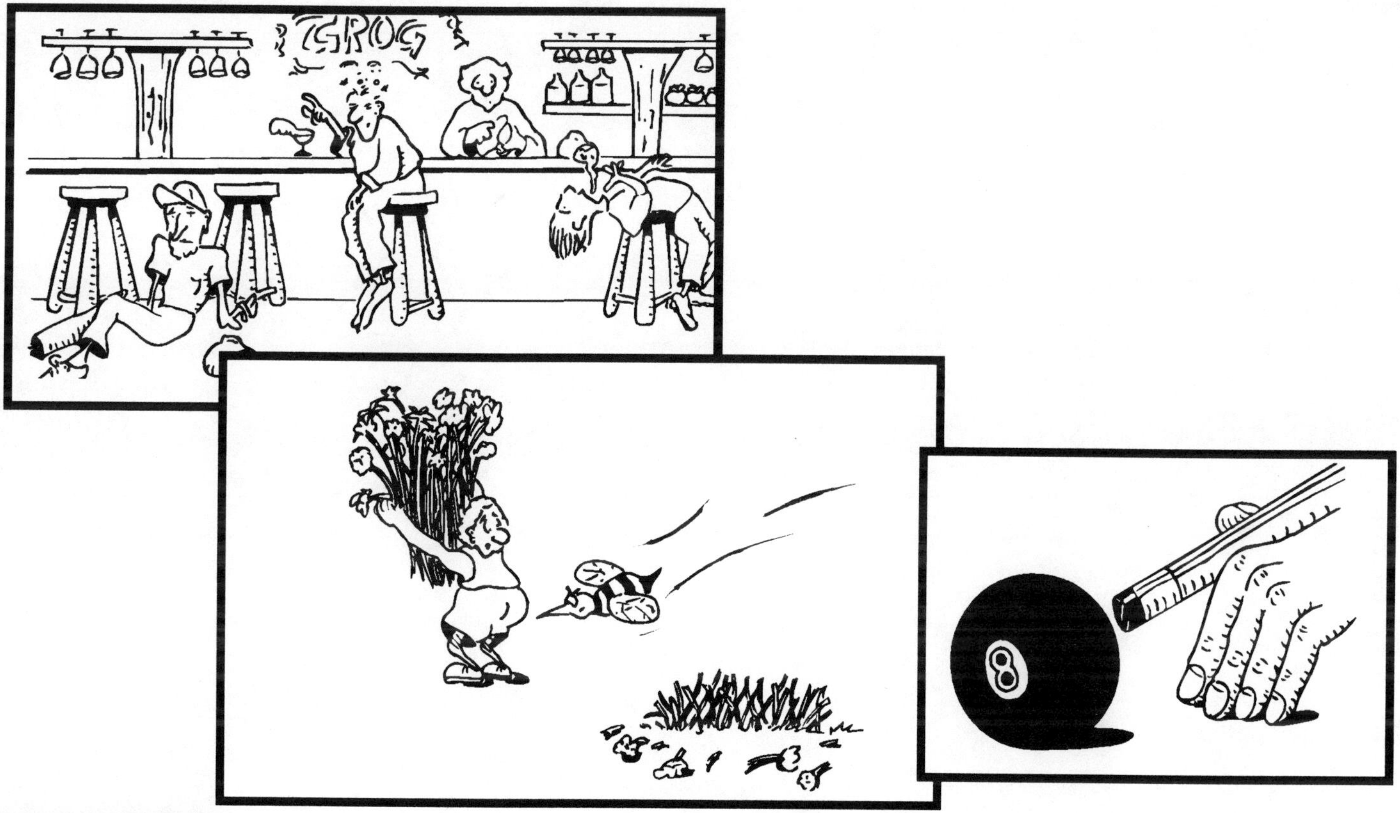
GROG
8

ANSWER ON BACK

BARBEQUE

8

Every State has one

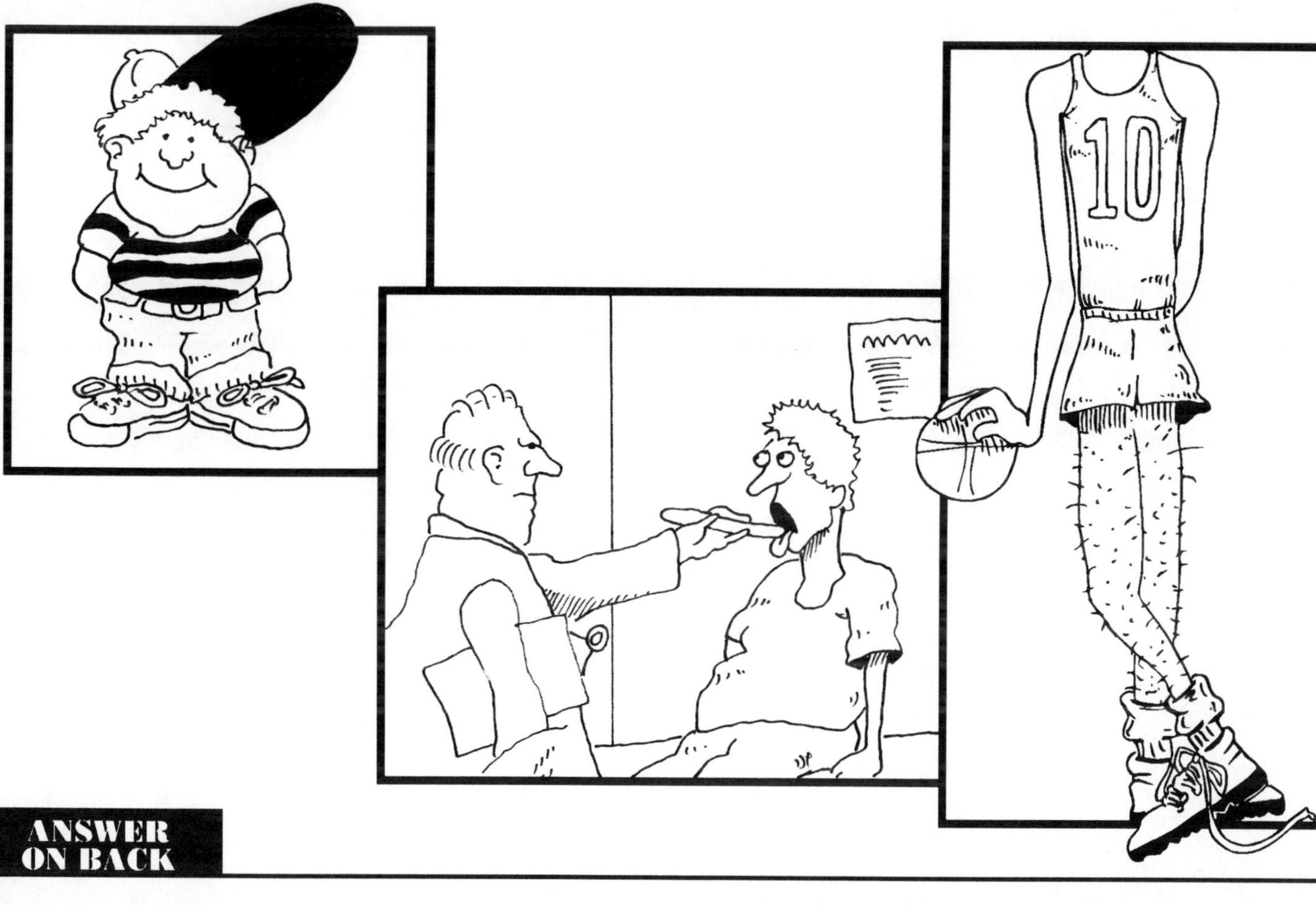
10

ANSWER ON BACK

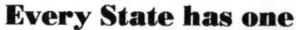

CAPITAL

9

When it's not plugged in

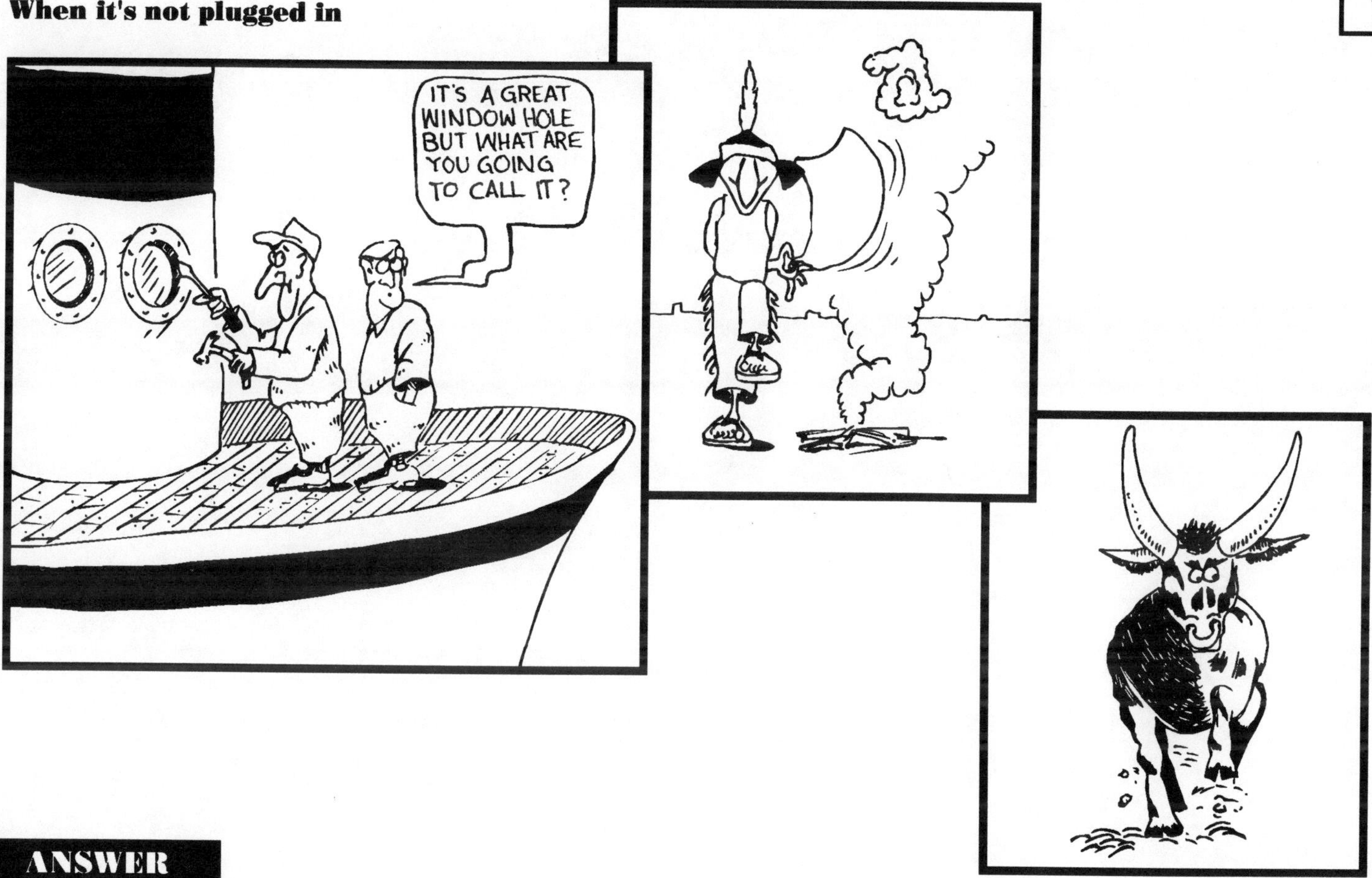
IT'S A GREAT WINDOW HOLE BUT WHAT ARE YOU GOING TO CALL IT?

ANSWER ON BACK

PORTABLE

The cause of Nielsen's ratings

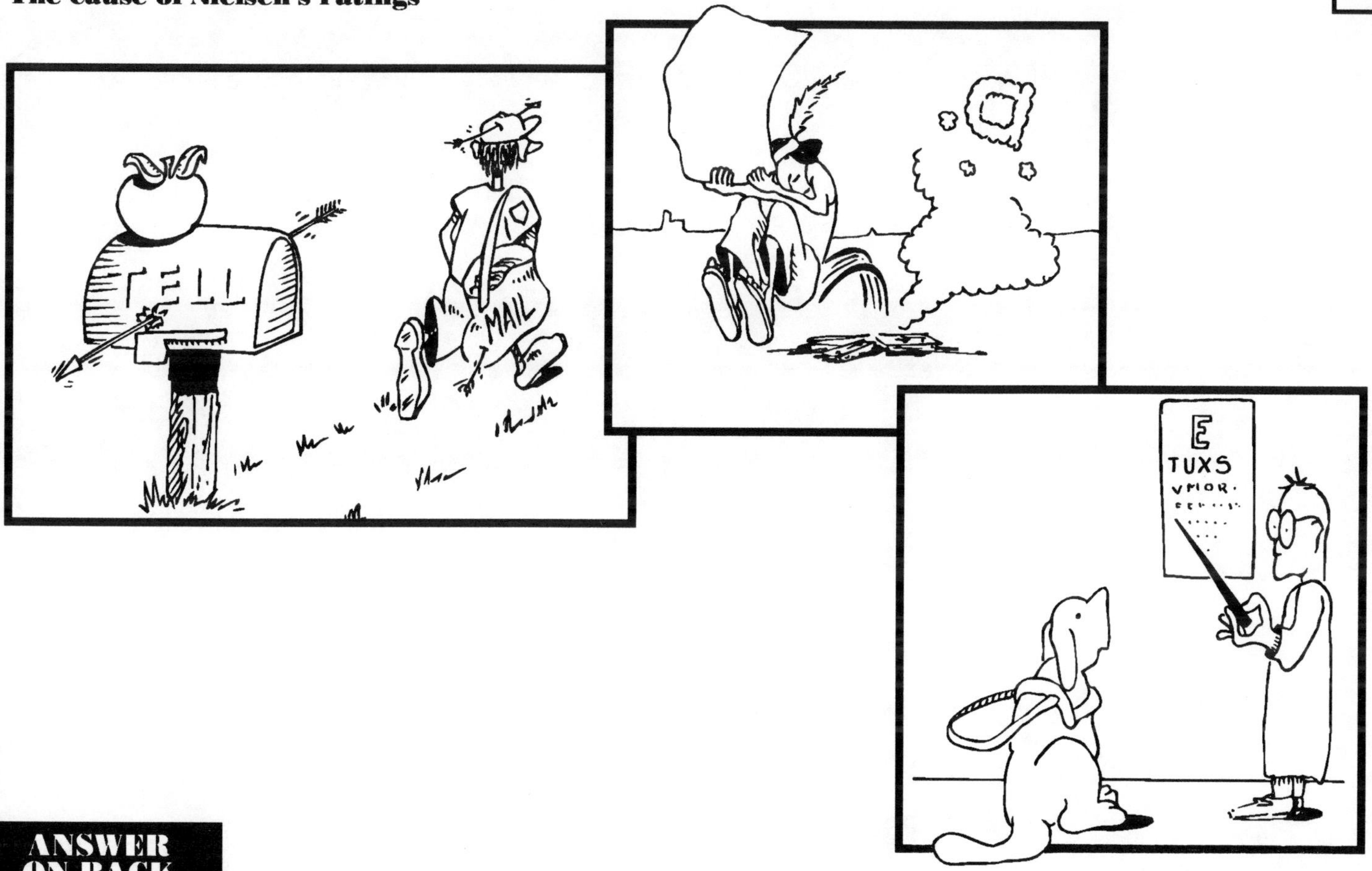
TELL
MAIL
E
TUXS
VMOR

ANSWER ON BACK

TELEVISION

Column of Personal Forecast.

ANSWER ON BACK

HOROSCOPE

What children seldom take

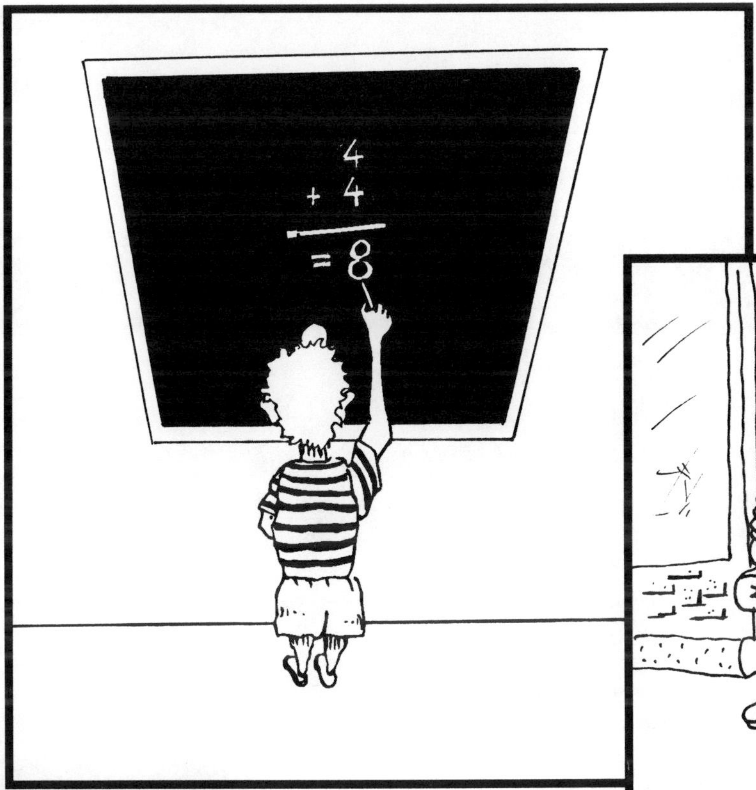
4
+ 4
= 8

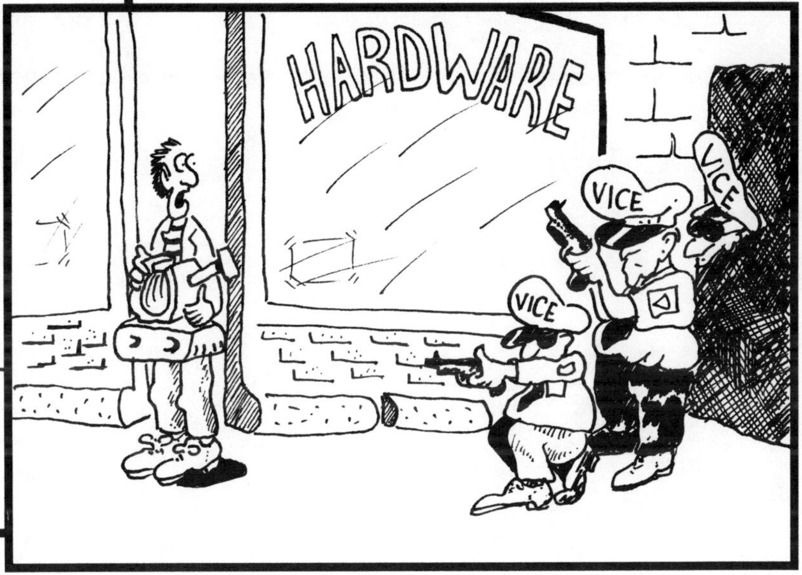
HARDWARE
VICE
VICE
VICE

ANSWER ON BACK

ADVICE

13

Bankers foot style

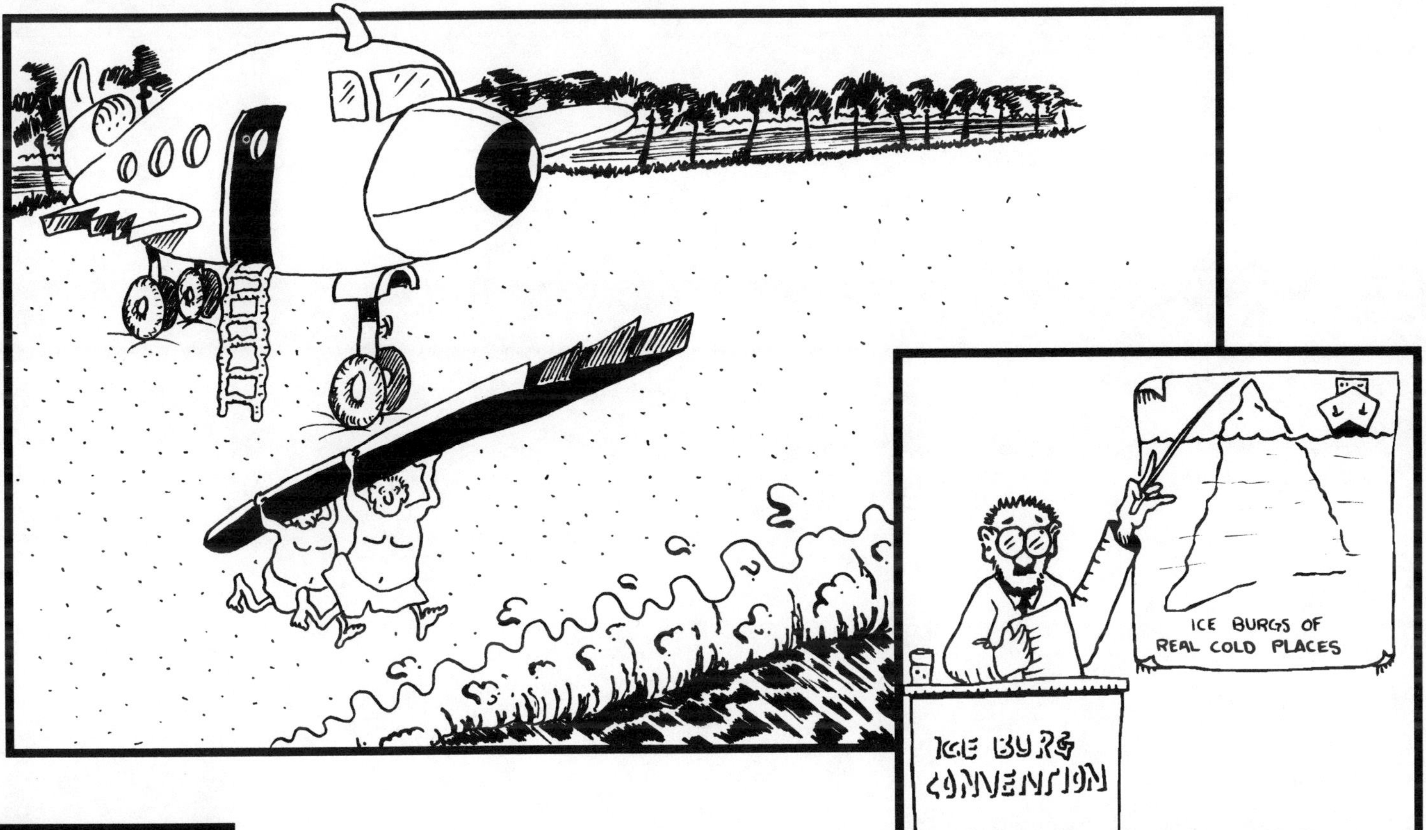
ICE BURGS OF
REAL COLD PLACES
ICE BURG
CONVENTION

ANSWER ON BACK

WING TIP

Associated with the color yellow

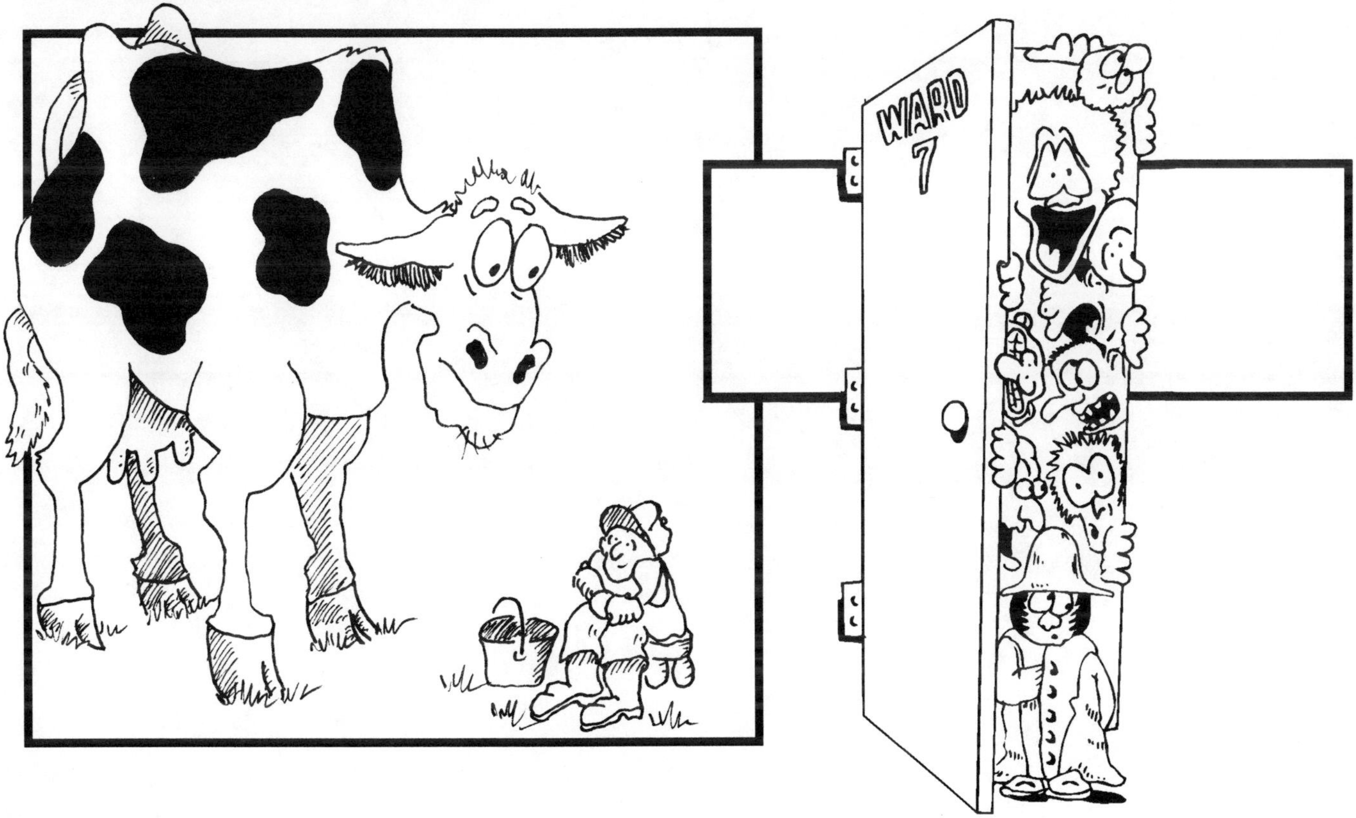
WARD
7

ANSWER ON BACK

COWARD

Speech after the dentist's novocain

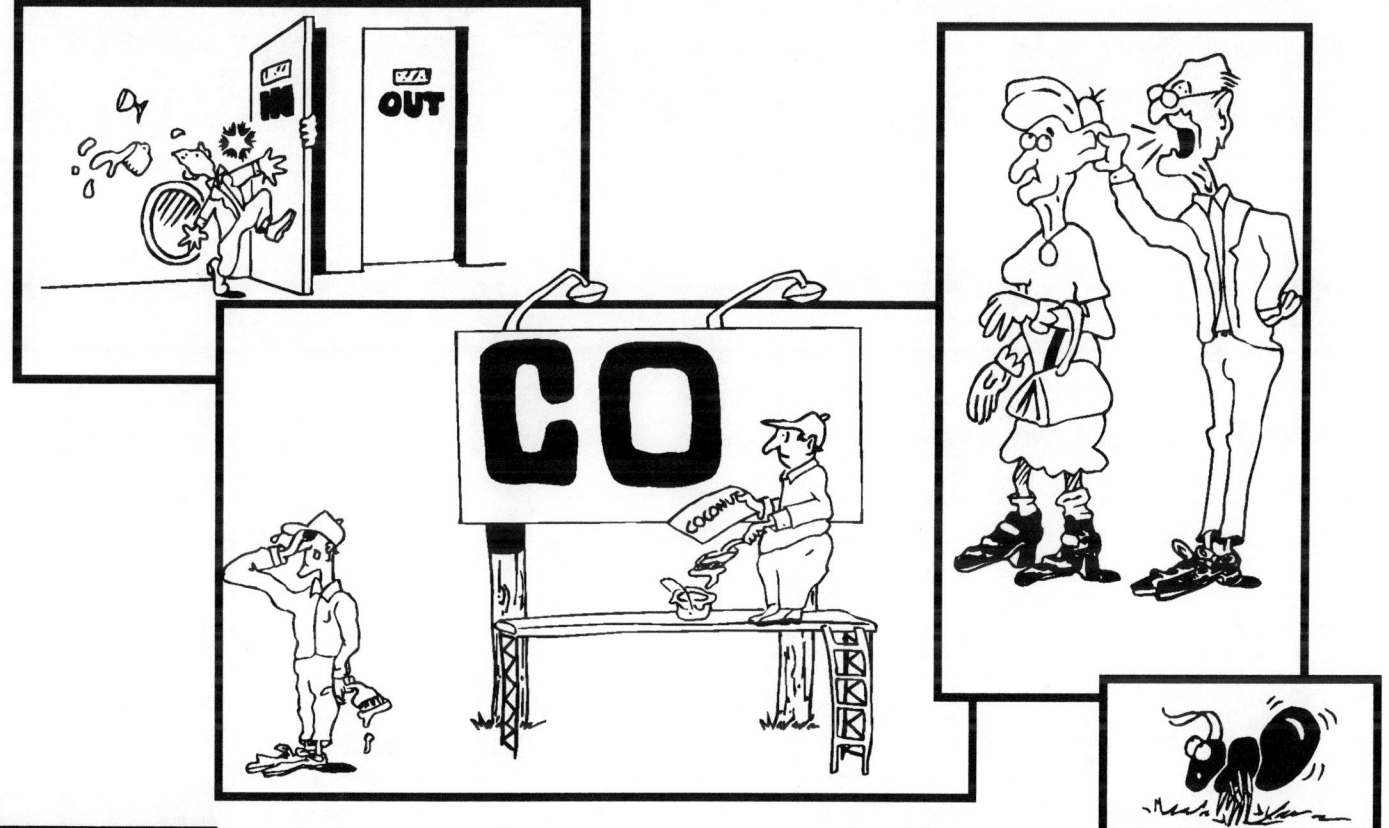

ANSWER
ON BACK

INCOHERENT

16

Runs at weddings

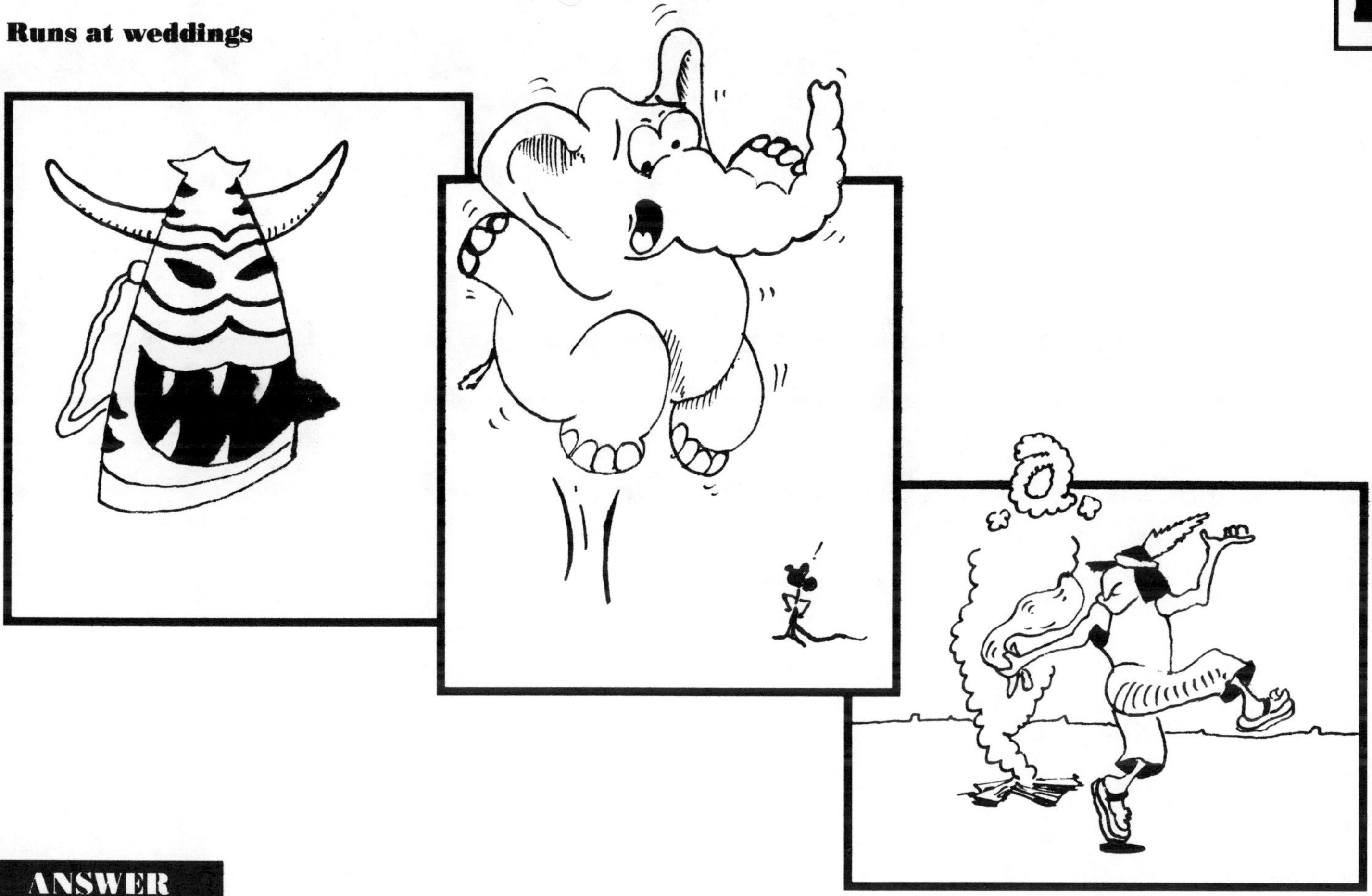

ANSWER ON BACK

MASCARA

Role model for: NEVER TELL A LIE

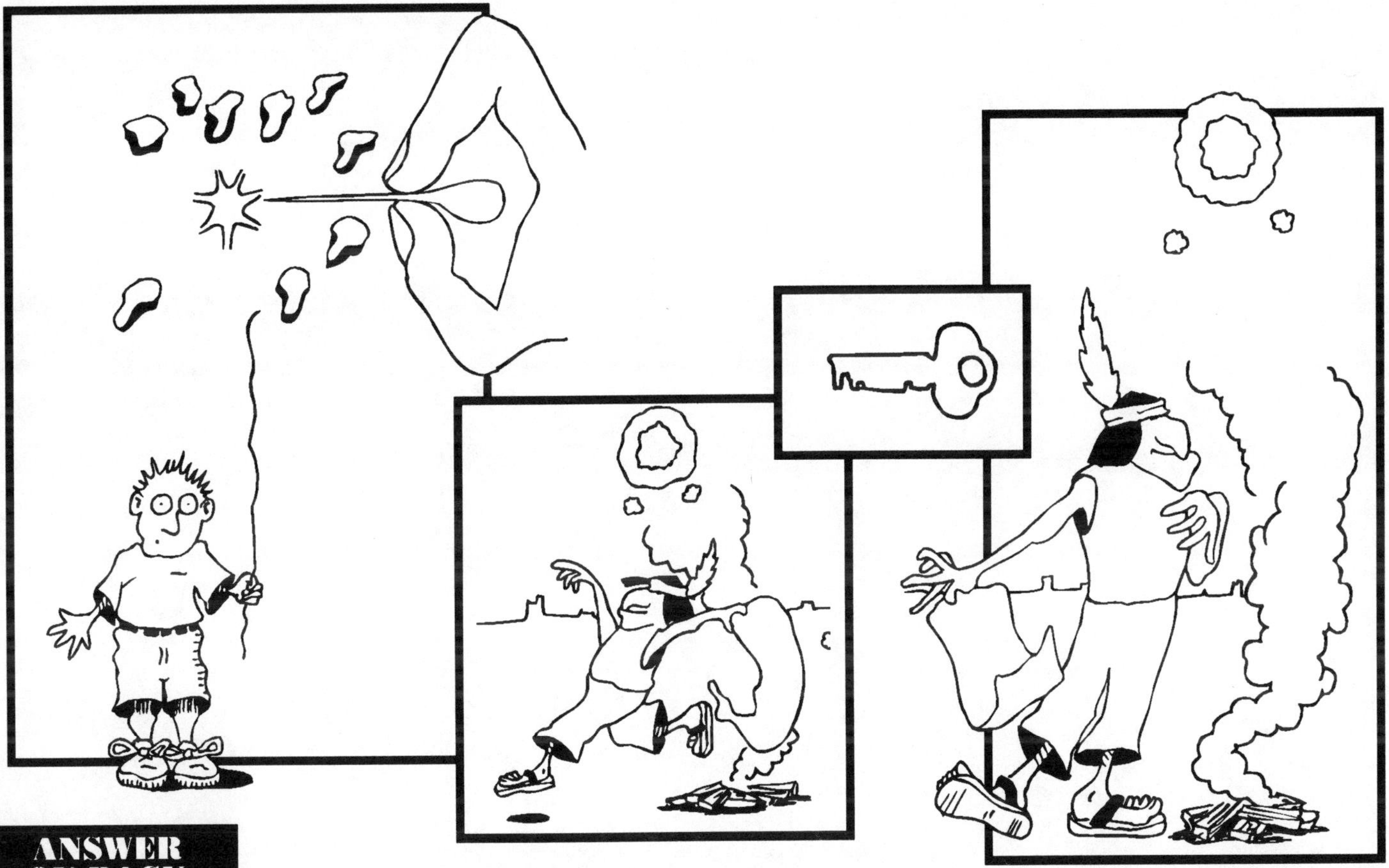

ANSWER ON BACK

PINOCCHIO

18

Dr. Kildare's student

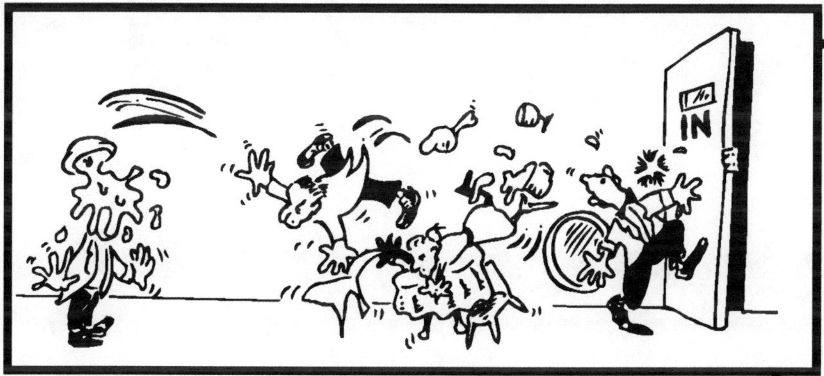

IN

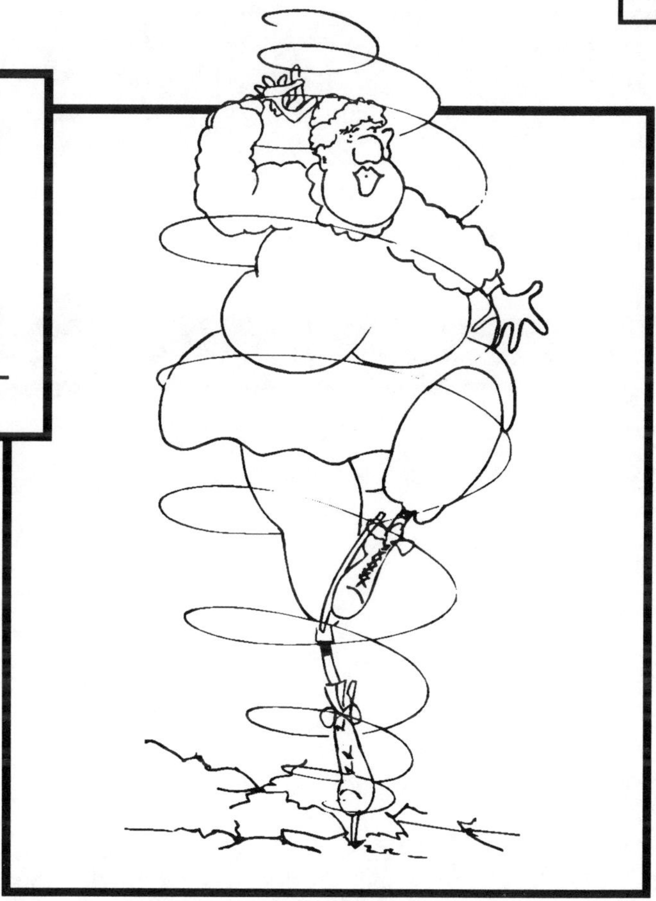

ANSWER ON BACK

INTERN

"To be or not to be", that is the question

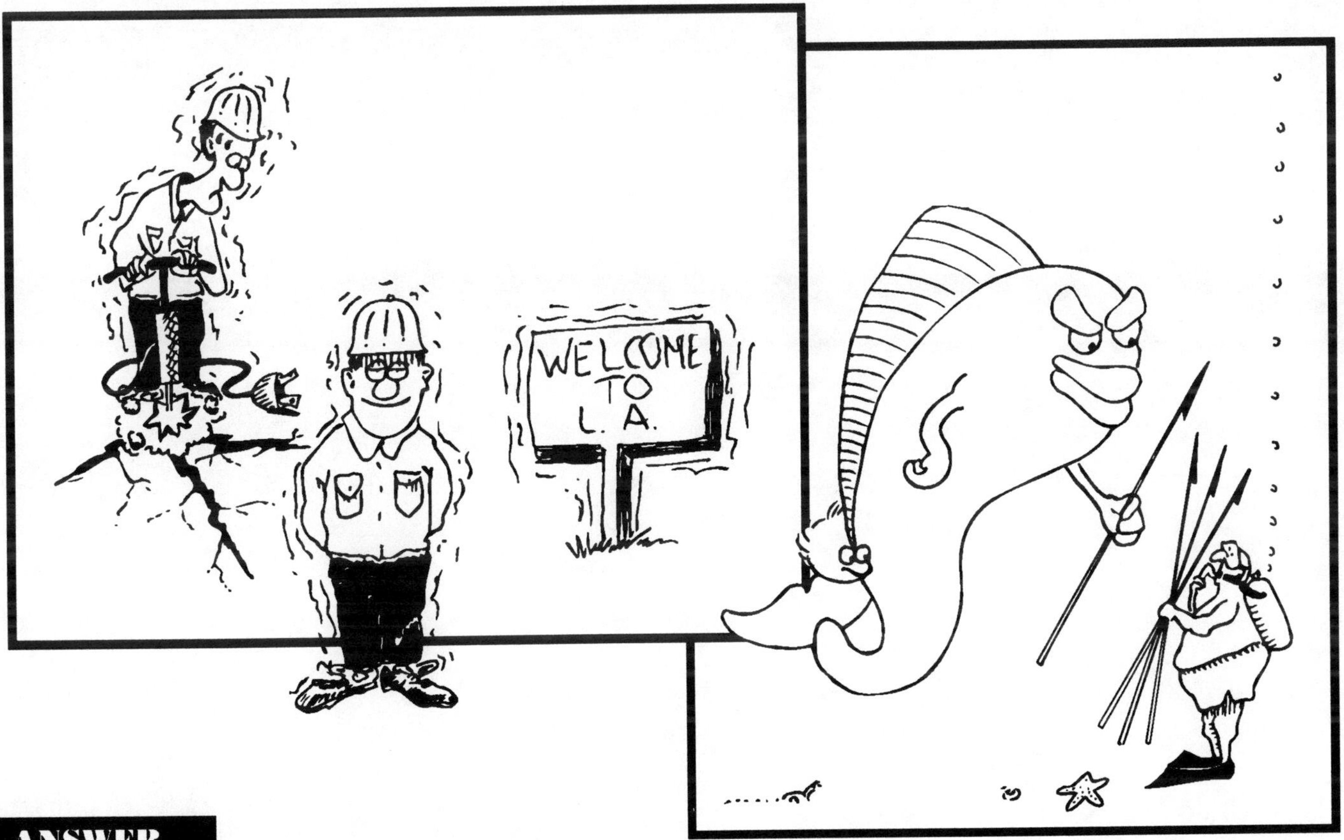
WELCOME TO L.A.

ANSWER ON BACK

SHAKESPEARE

Why tourists crane their necks

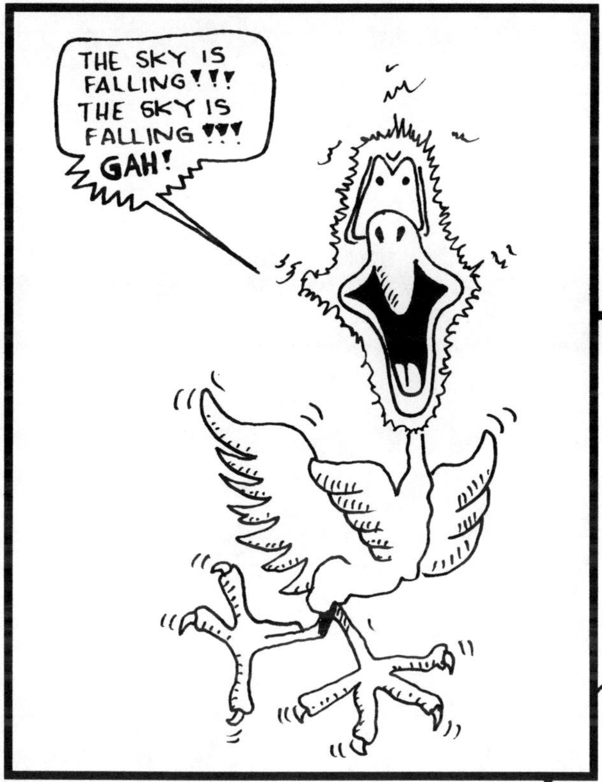
THE SKY IS FALLING!!!
THE SKY IS FALLING!!!
GAH!

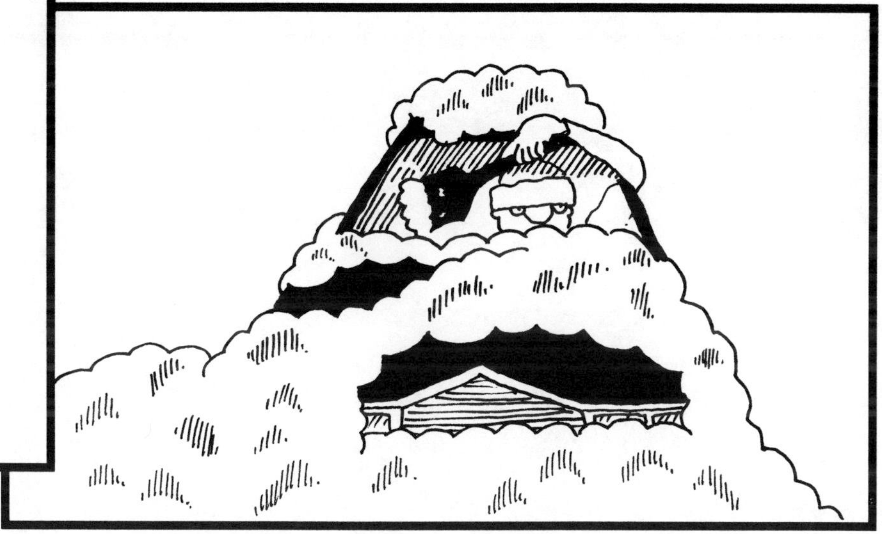

ANSWER ON BACK

SKYSCRAPER

A "dish" made from a rib

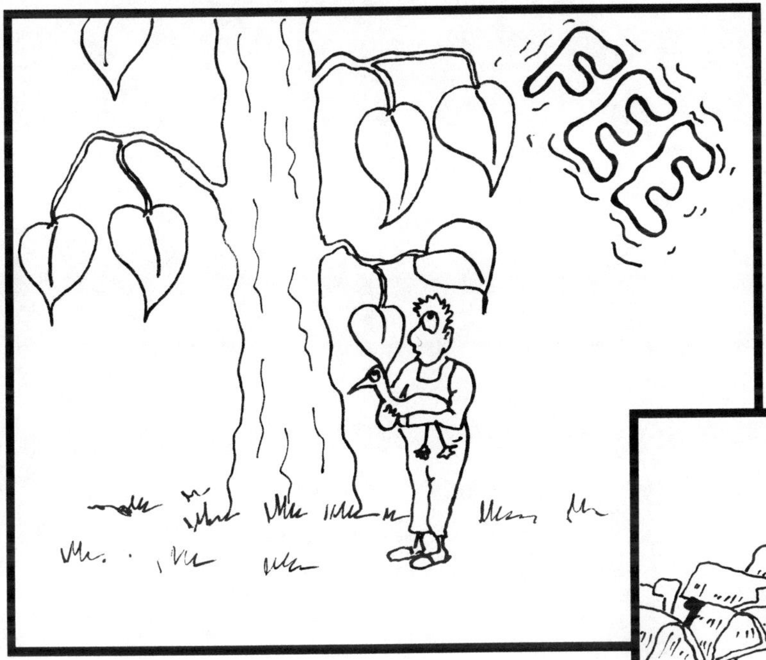
FEE

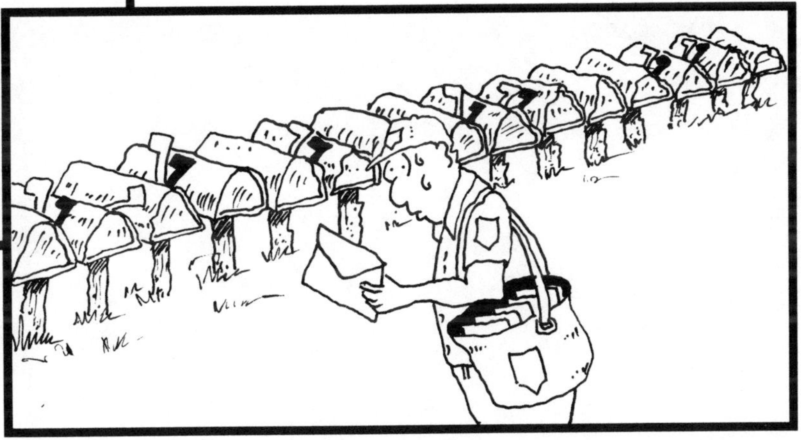

ANSWER ON BACK

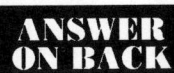

FEMALE

22

Making disappear

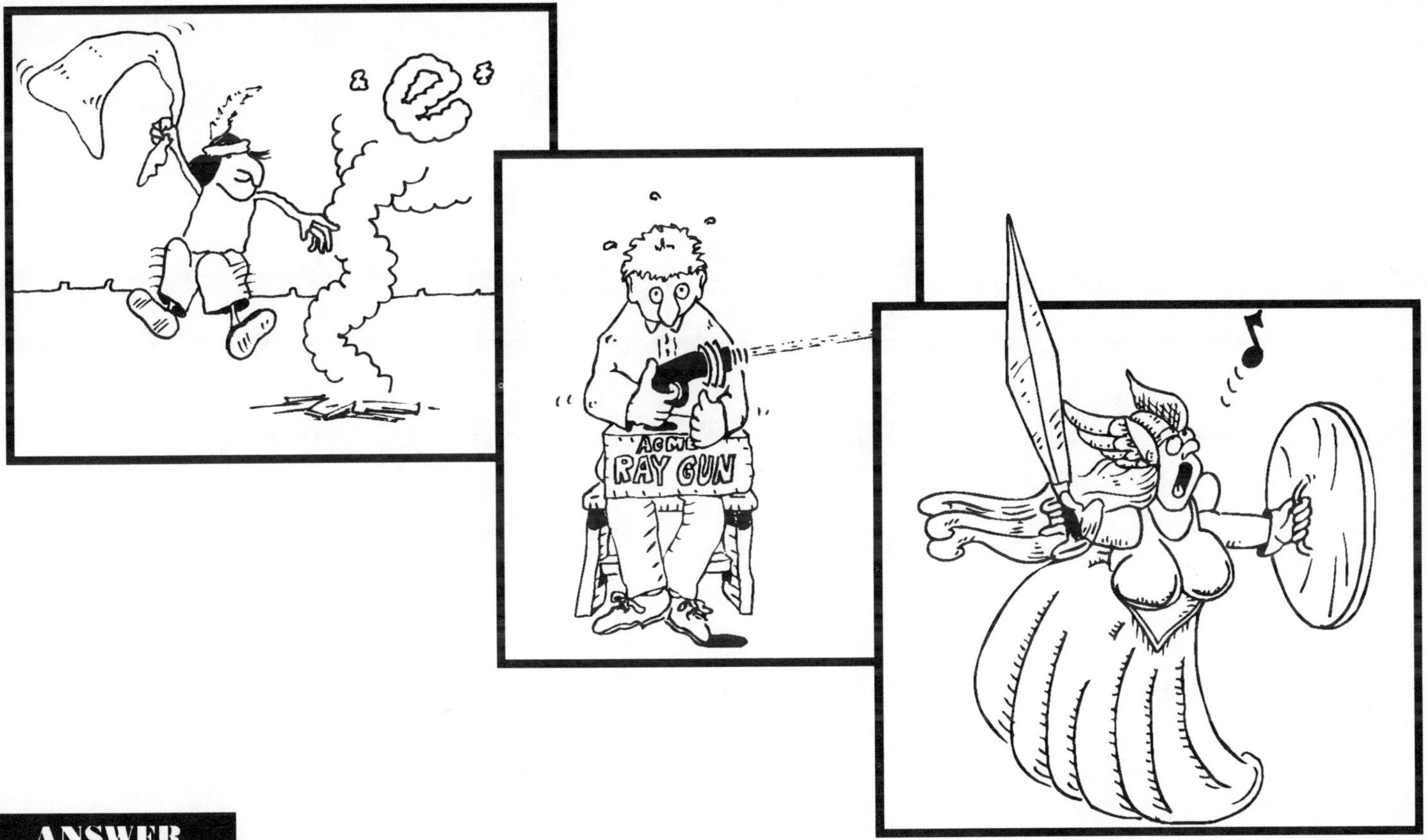
ACME
RAY GUN

ANSWER ON BACK

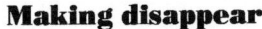

ERASING

What Sitting Bull yelled when he saw Custer

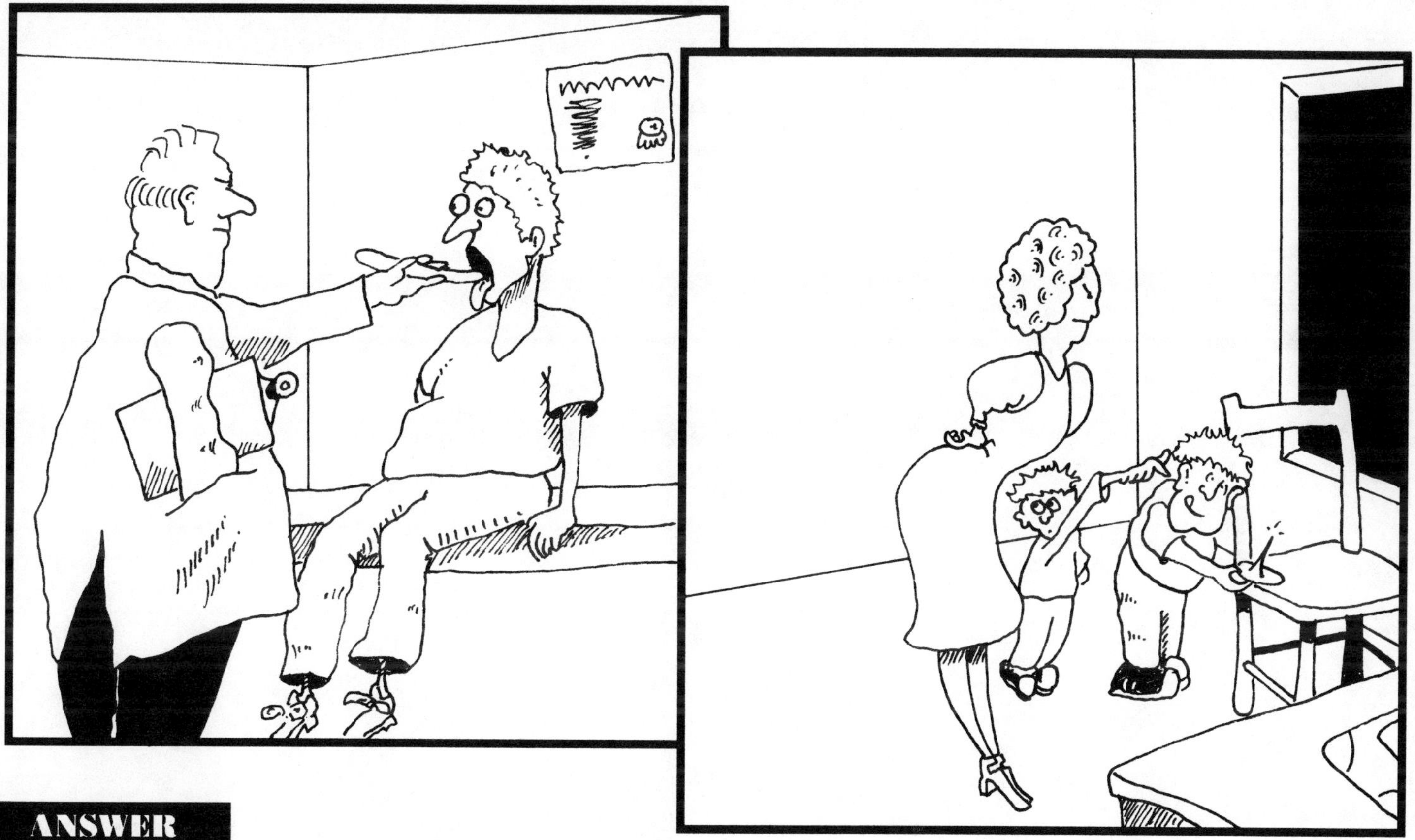

ANSWER ON BACK

ATTACK

24

Adjective for "THE OLD EASY CHAIR"

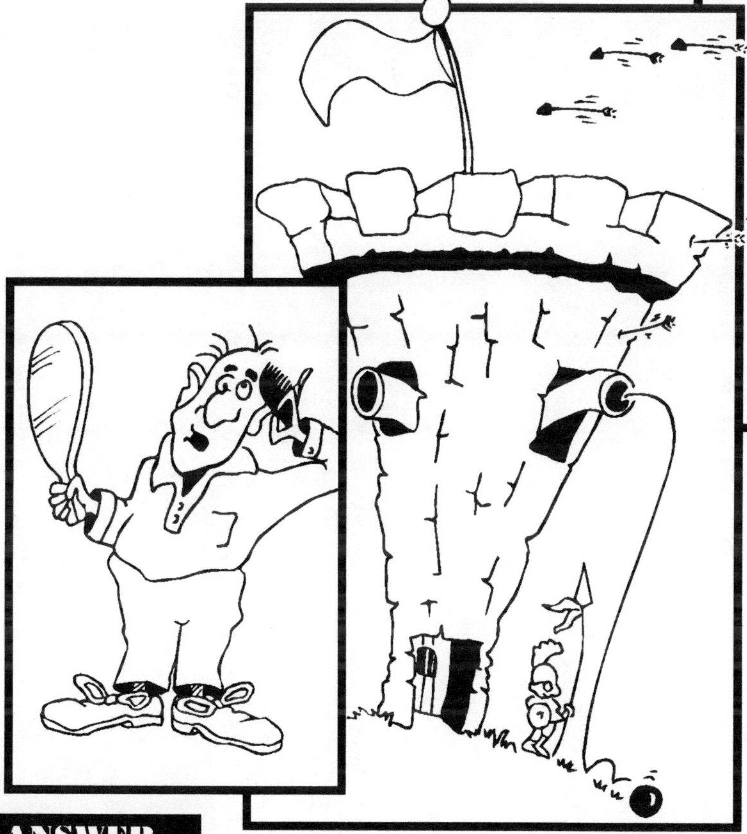

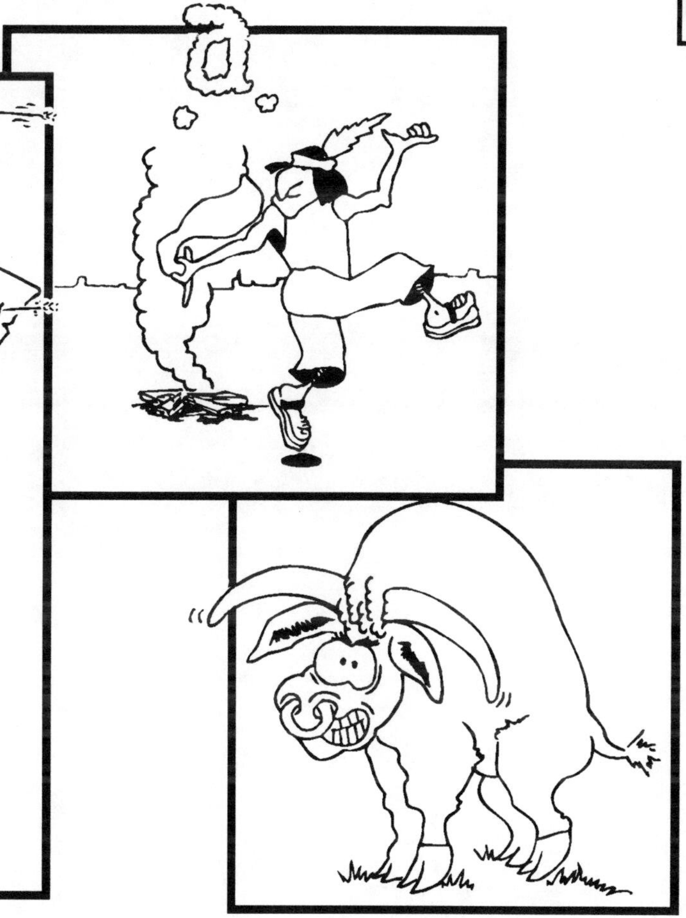
a

ANSWER ON BACK

COMFORTABLE

"Very" below average

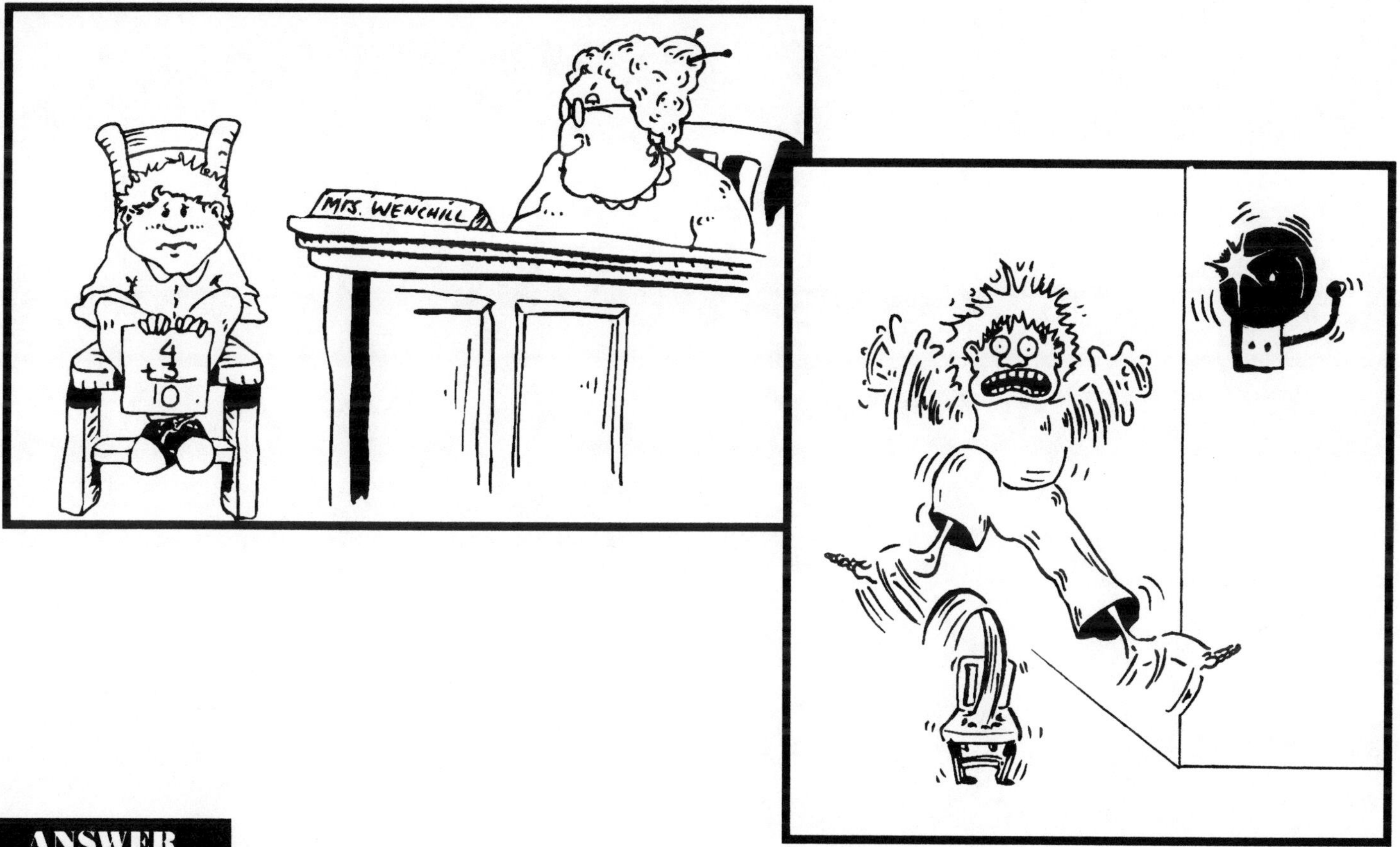
MRS. WENCHILL
4
+3
10

ANSWER ON BACK

DUMBBELL

26

Television star played by the largest cousin of the deer family.

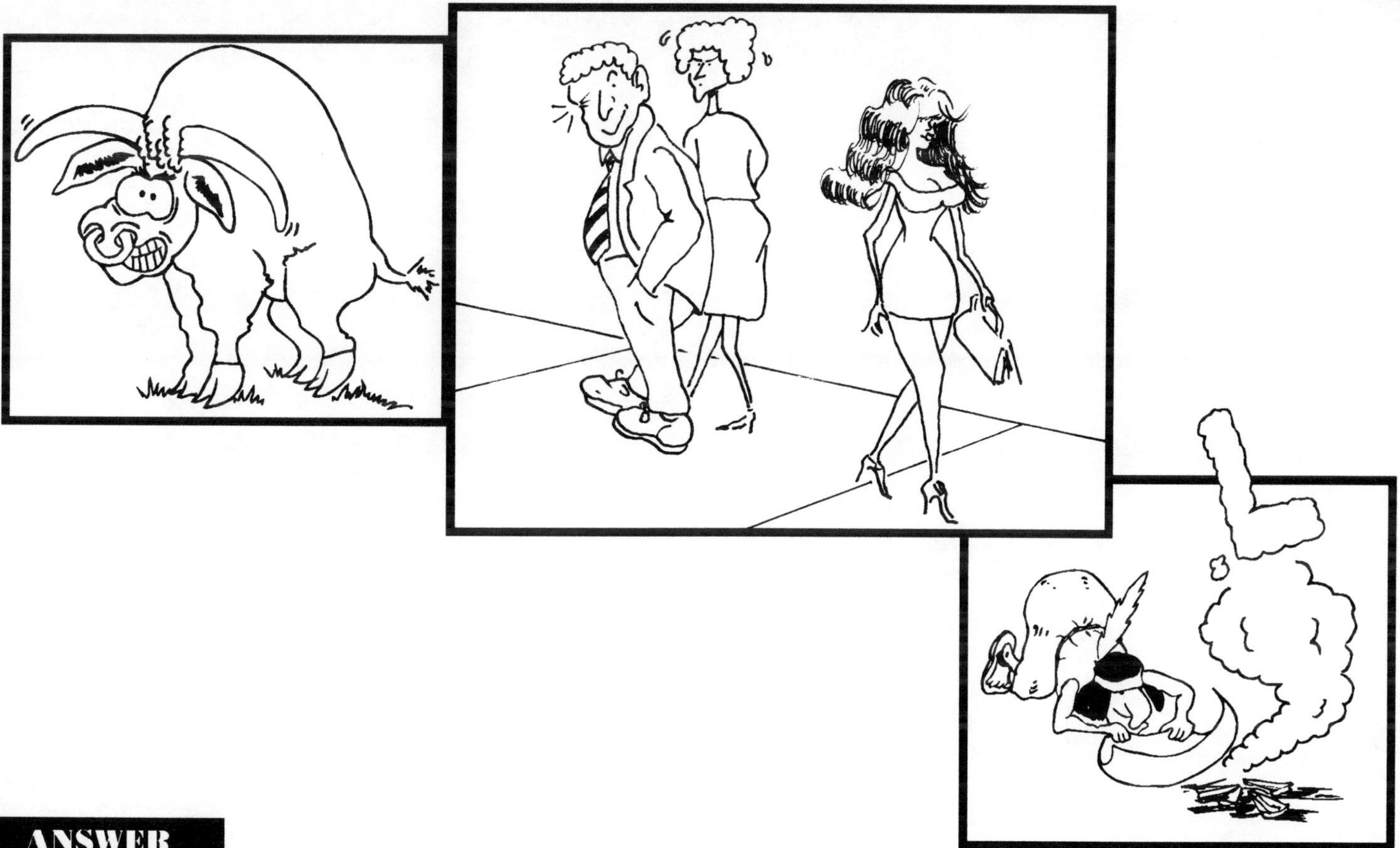

ANSWER ON BACK

BULLWINKLE

27

What the Minister gives his flock

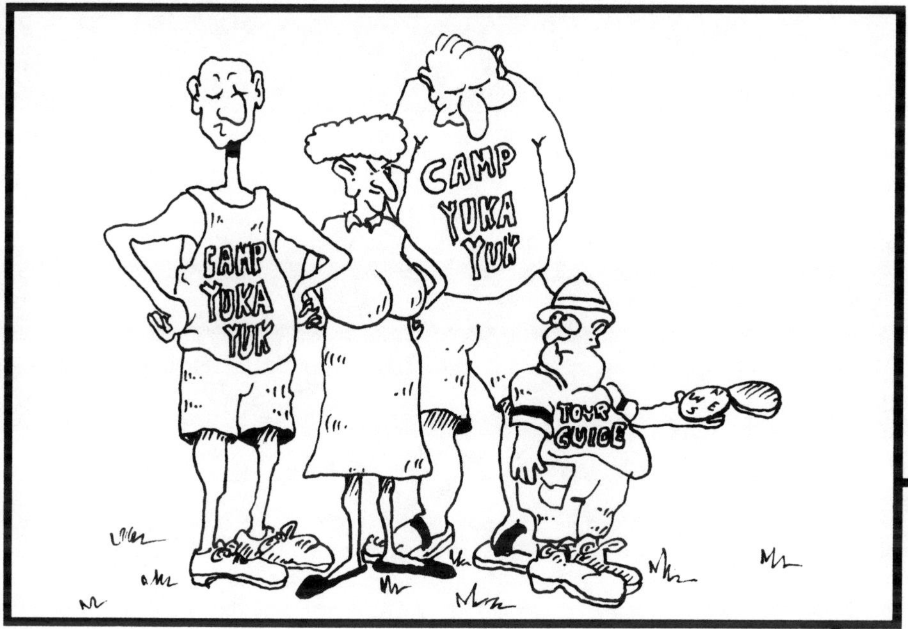
CAMP
YUKA
YUK
CAMP
YUKA
YUK
TOUR
GUIDE

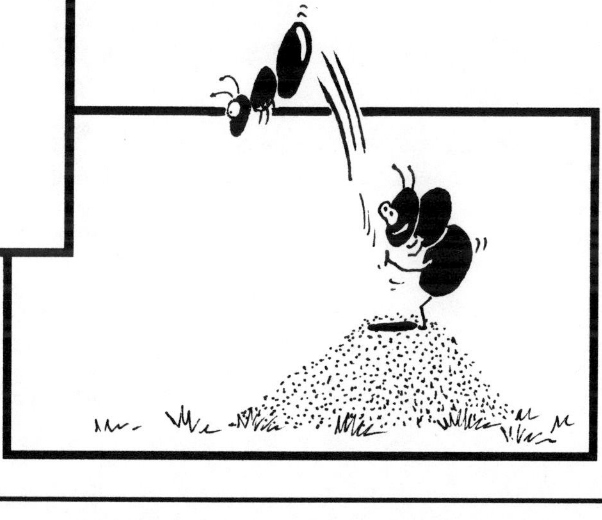

ANSWER ON BACK

GUIDANCE

What a lonely person desires

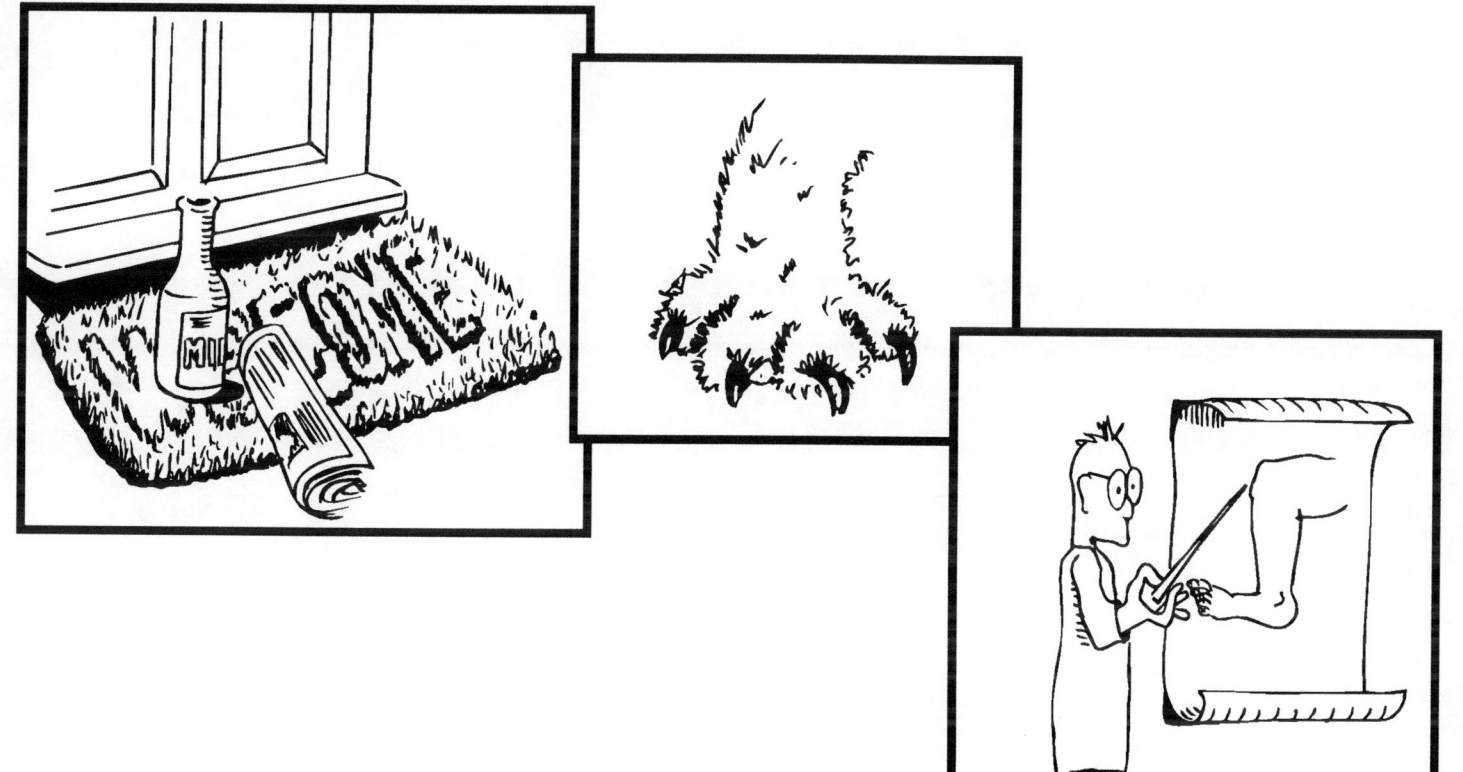

ANSWER ON BACK

COMPANY

Producer of fast foods

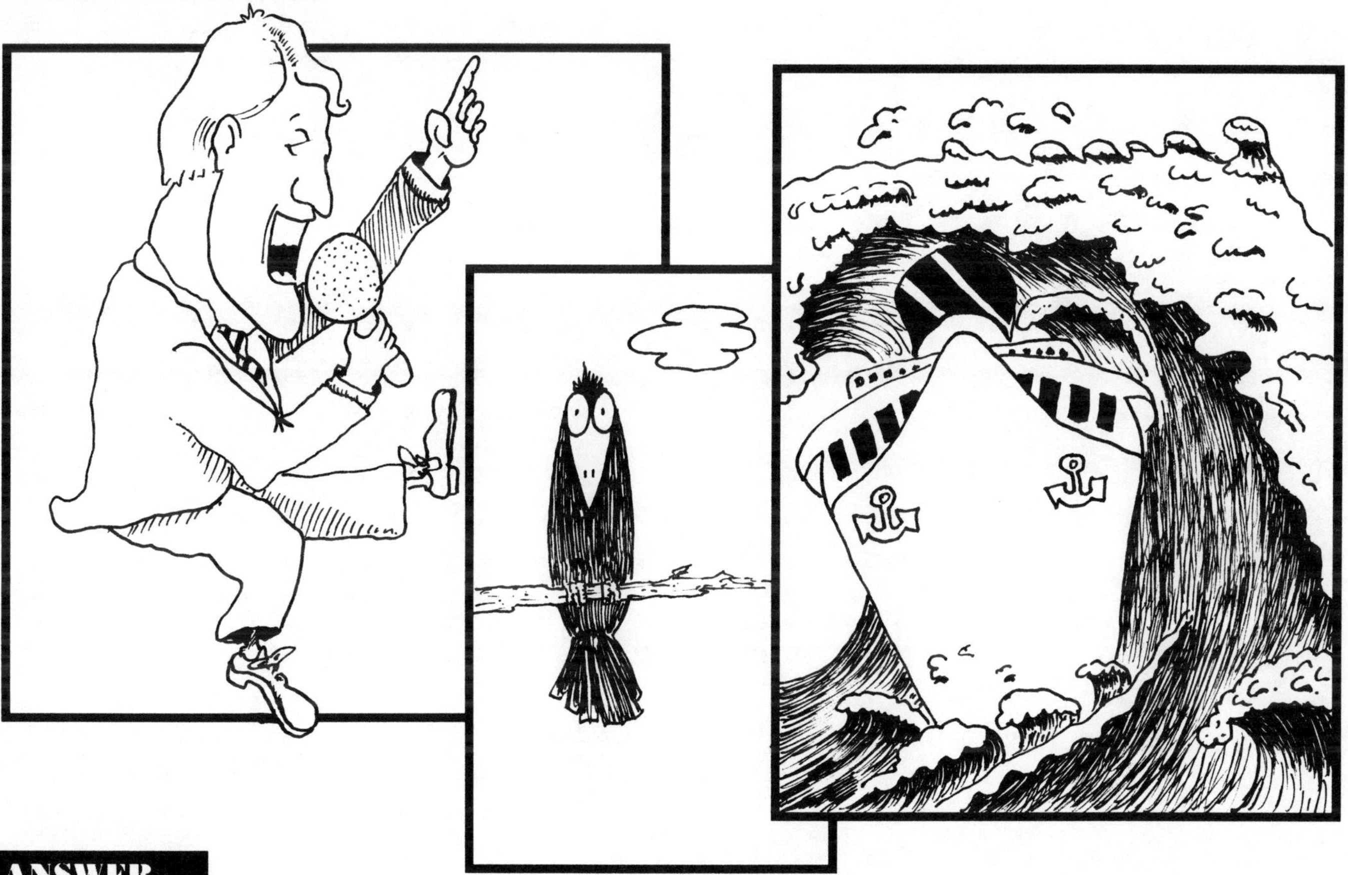

ANSWER ON BACK

MICROWAVE

A common Ghost Town Prop

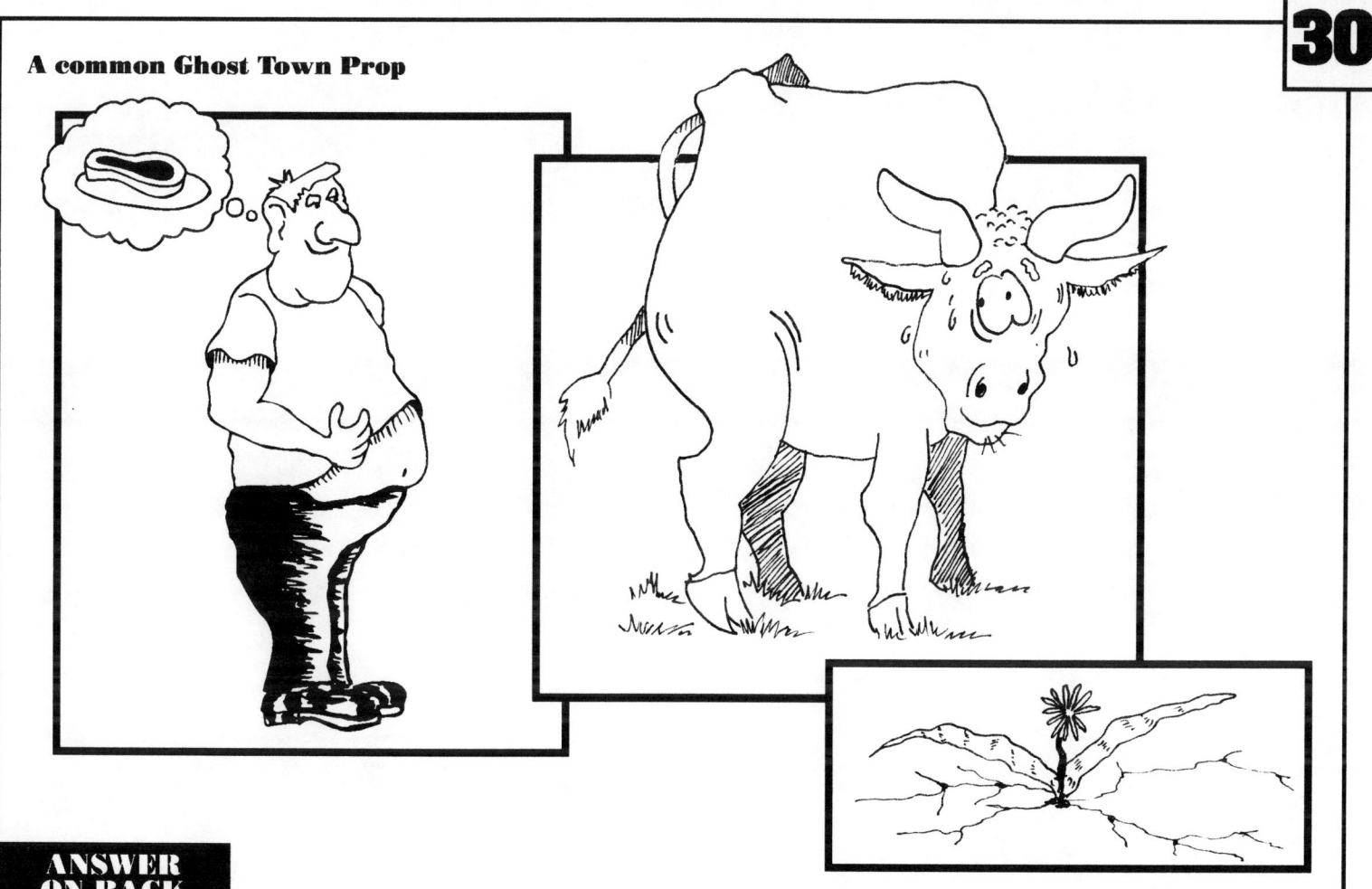

ANSWER ON BACK

TUMBLEWEED

31

What the braggart is full of

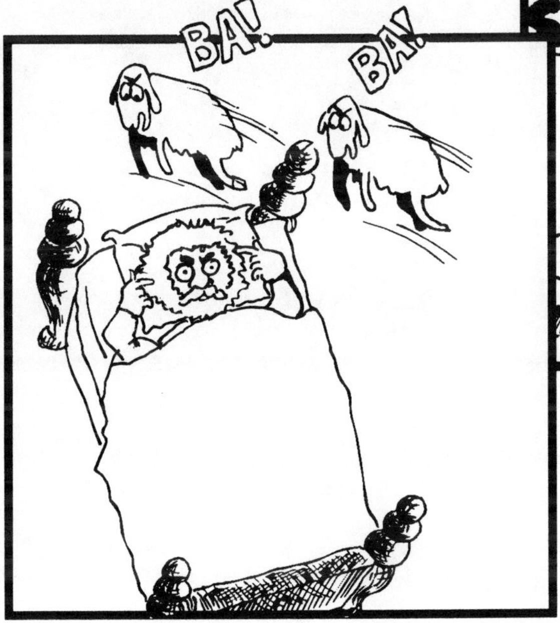
BA!
BA!

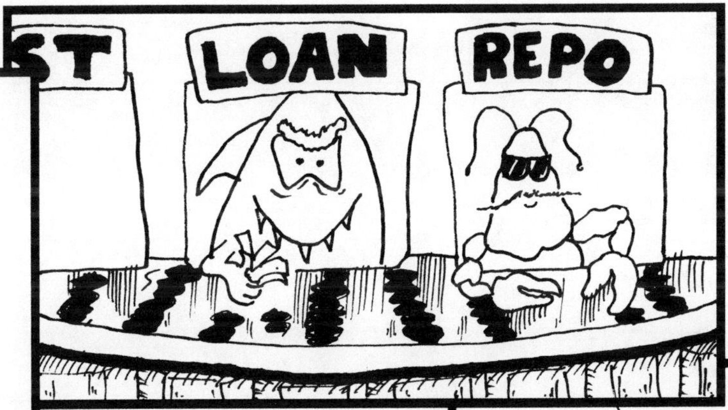
ST
LOAN
REPO

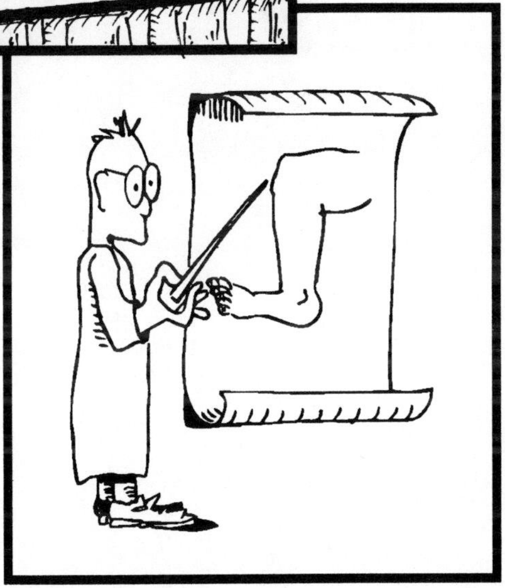

ANSWER ON BACK

BOLOGNA

Classic transportation of the 40's

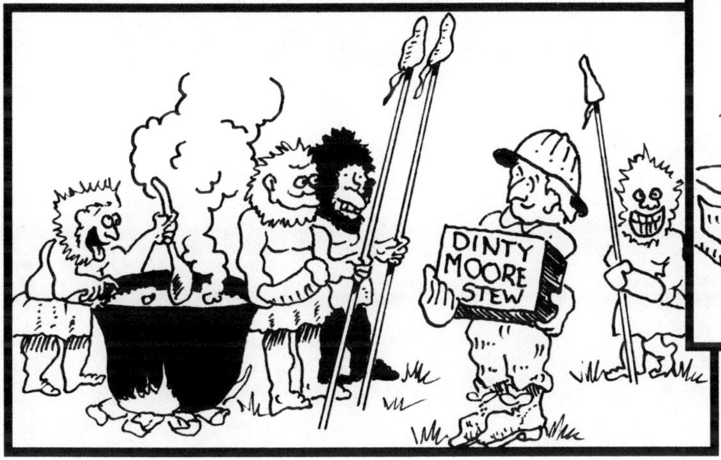
DINTY
MOORE
STEW

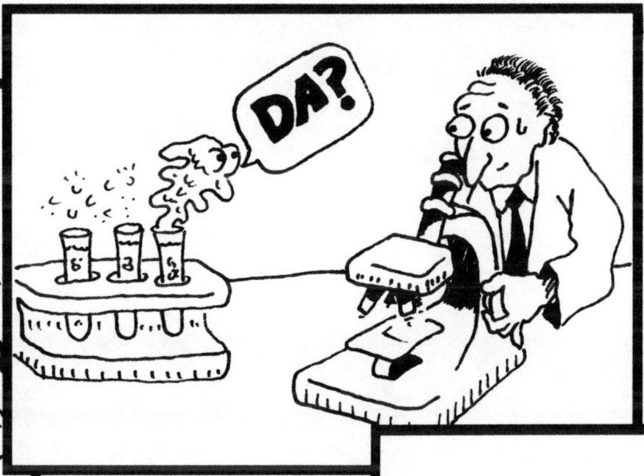
DA?

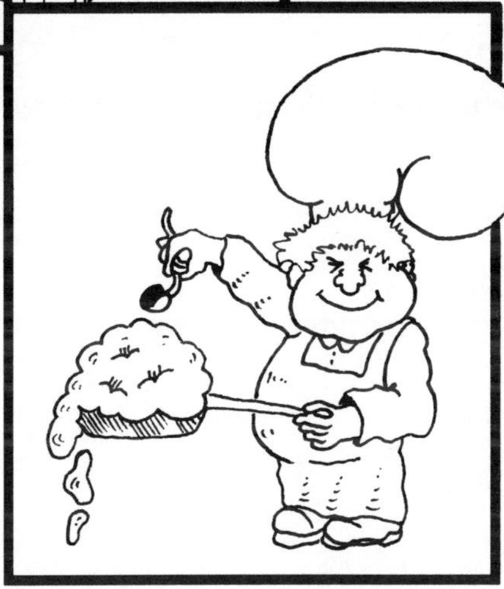

ANSWER ON BACK

STUDEBAKER

A Hollywood "bulls eye"

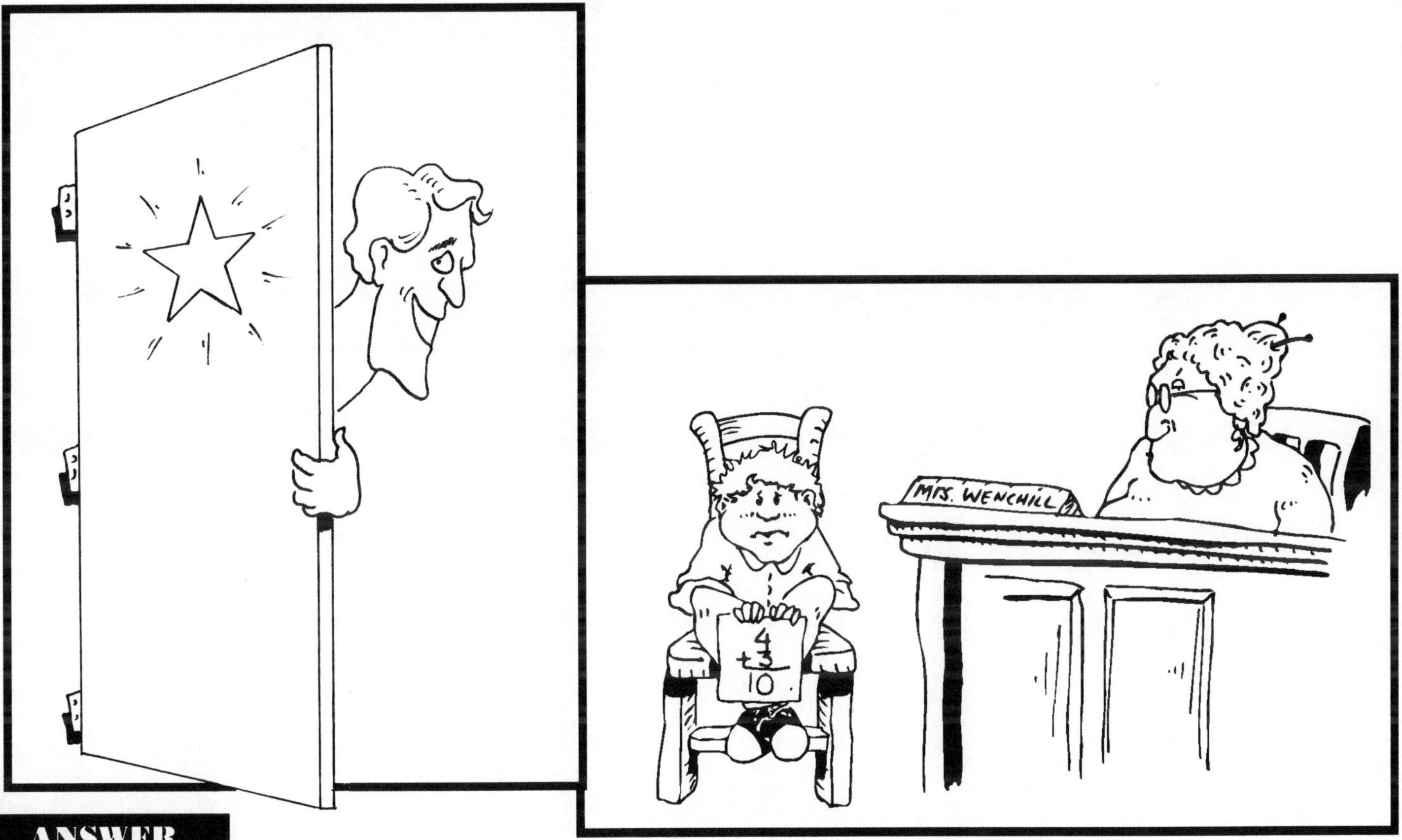
MRS. WENCHILL
4
+3
10

ANSWER ON BACK

STARDOM

A fruit that is neither of its parts

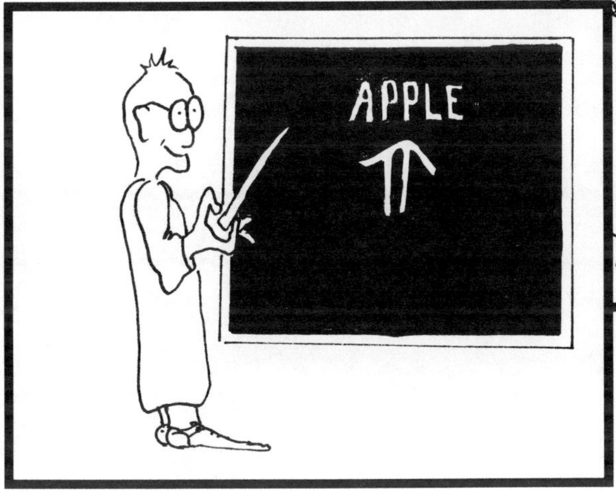
APPLE

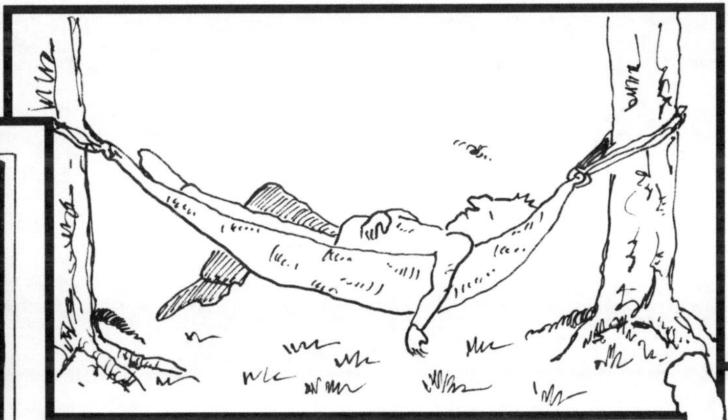

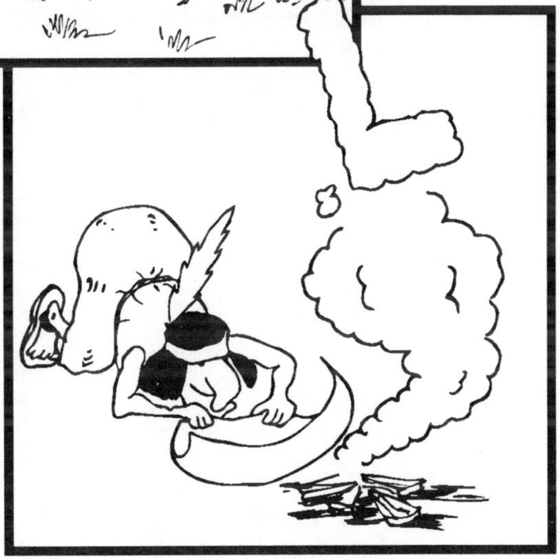

ANSWER ON BACK

PINEAPPLE

Very depressed by the ice age

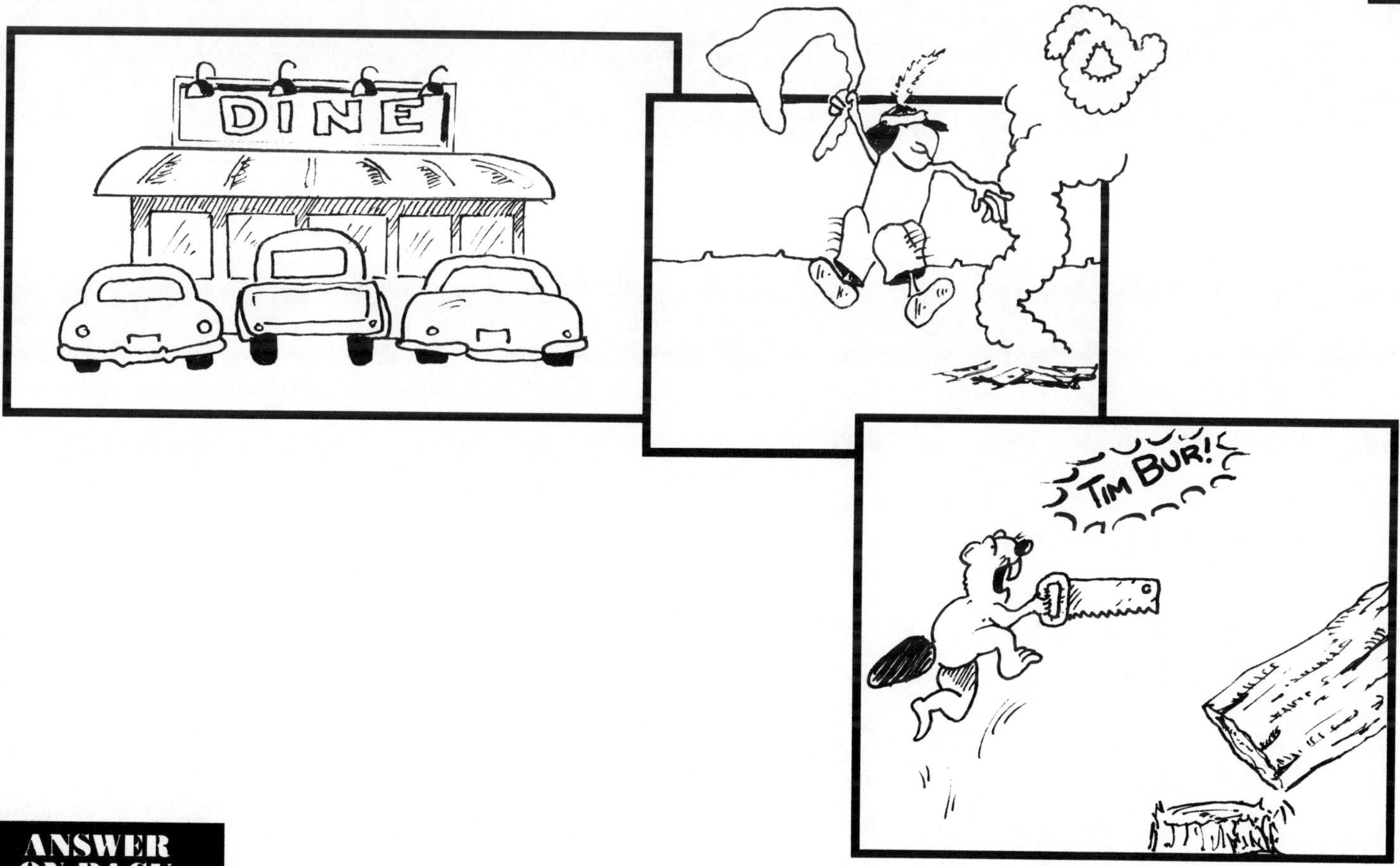

DINE
TIM BUR!

ANSWER ON BACK

DINOSAUR

Ammunition for an Amorous Ambush

ANSWER ON BACK

MISTLETOE

Concentrated scent

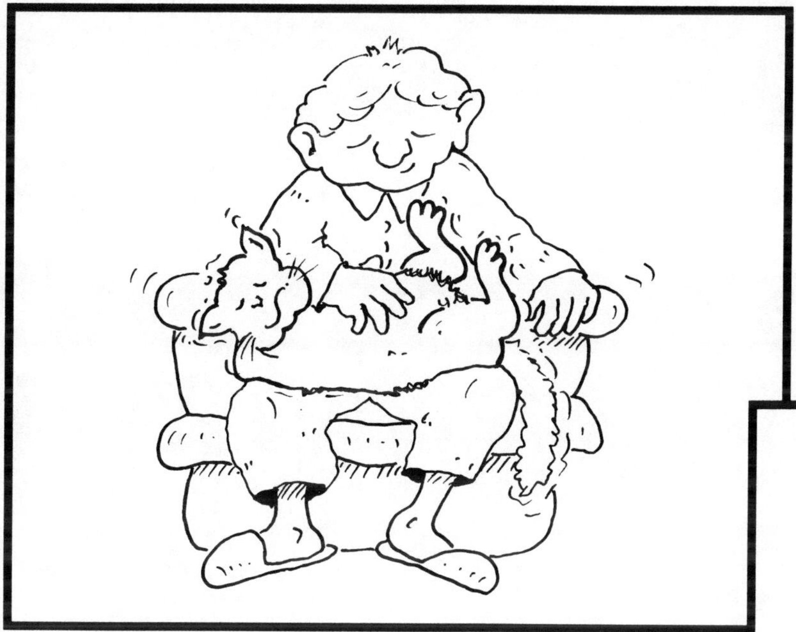

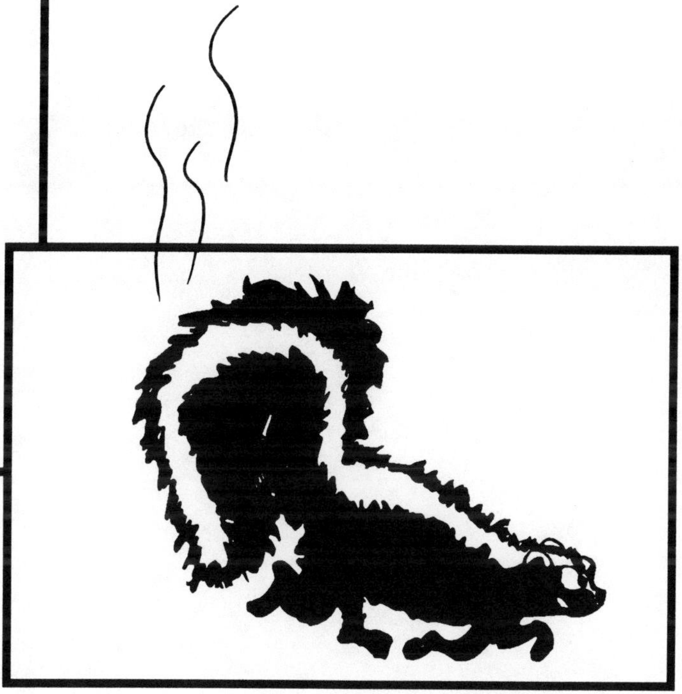

ANSWER ON BACK

PERFUME

To shrink

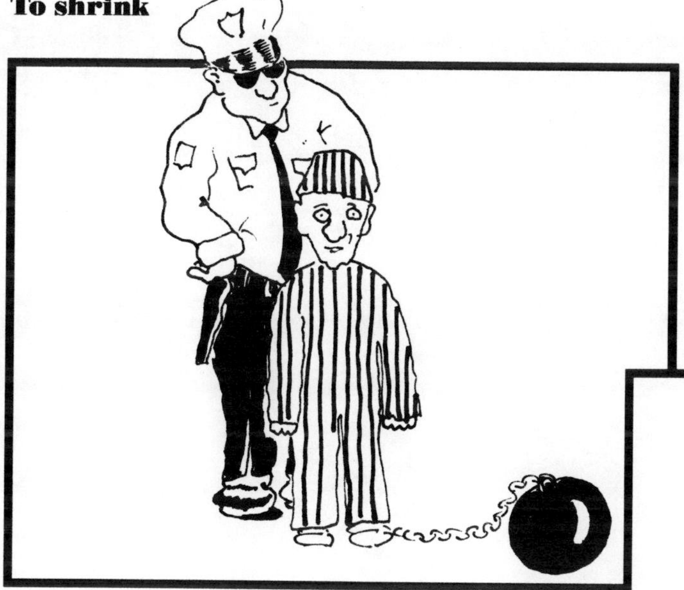

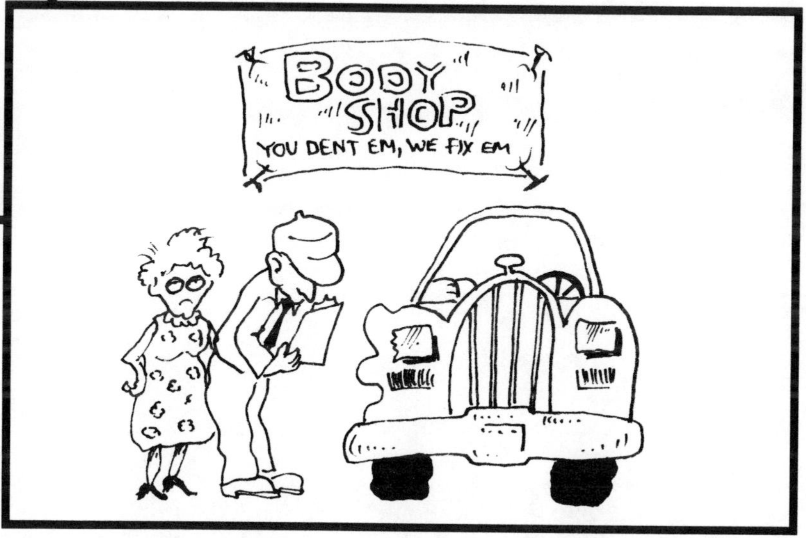
BODY SHOP
YOU DENT EM, WE FIX EM

ANSWER ON BACK

CONDENSE

39

Adjective for a Puppy

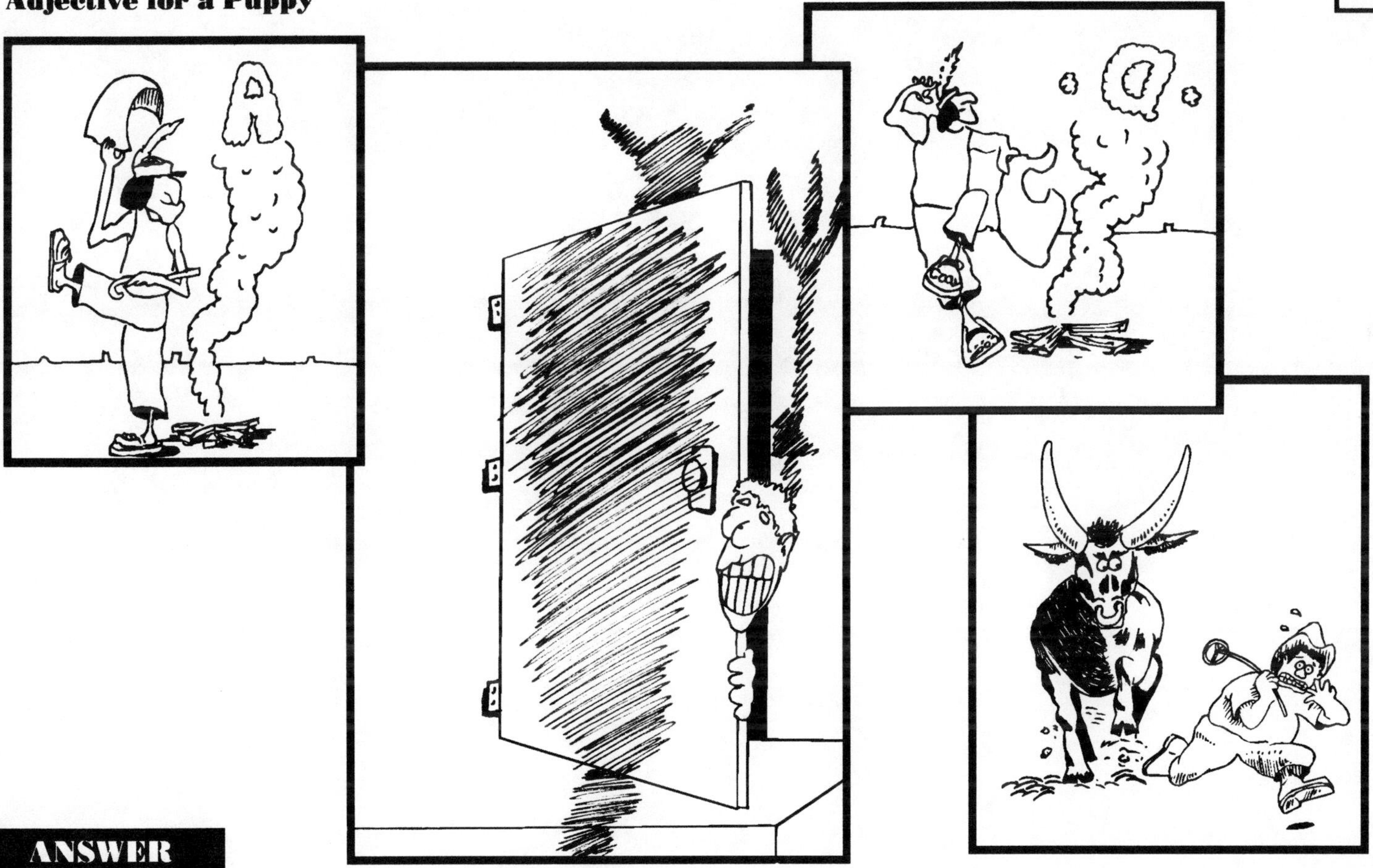
A
D

ANSWER ON BACK

ADORABLE

40

Commonly linked with the word "Foreign"

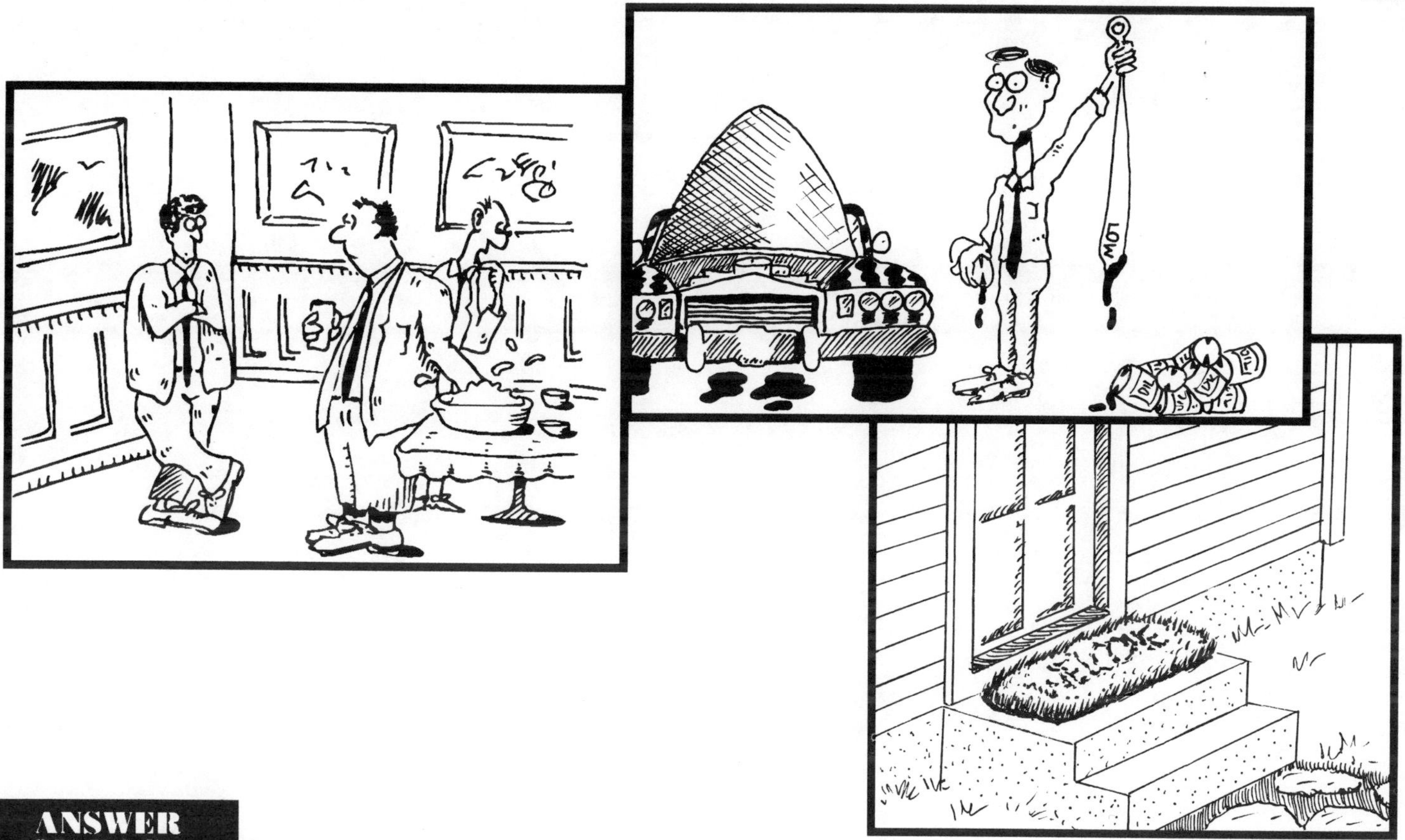
MOT
OIL

ANSWER ON BACK

DIPLOMAT

What advertisers put on strong cleaners

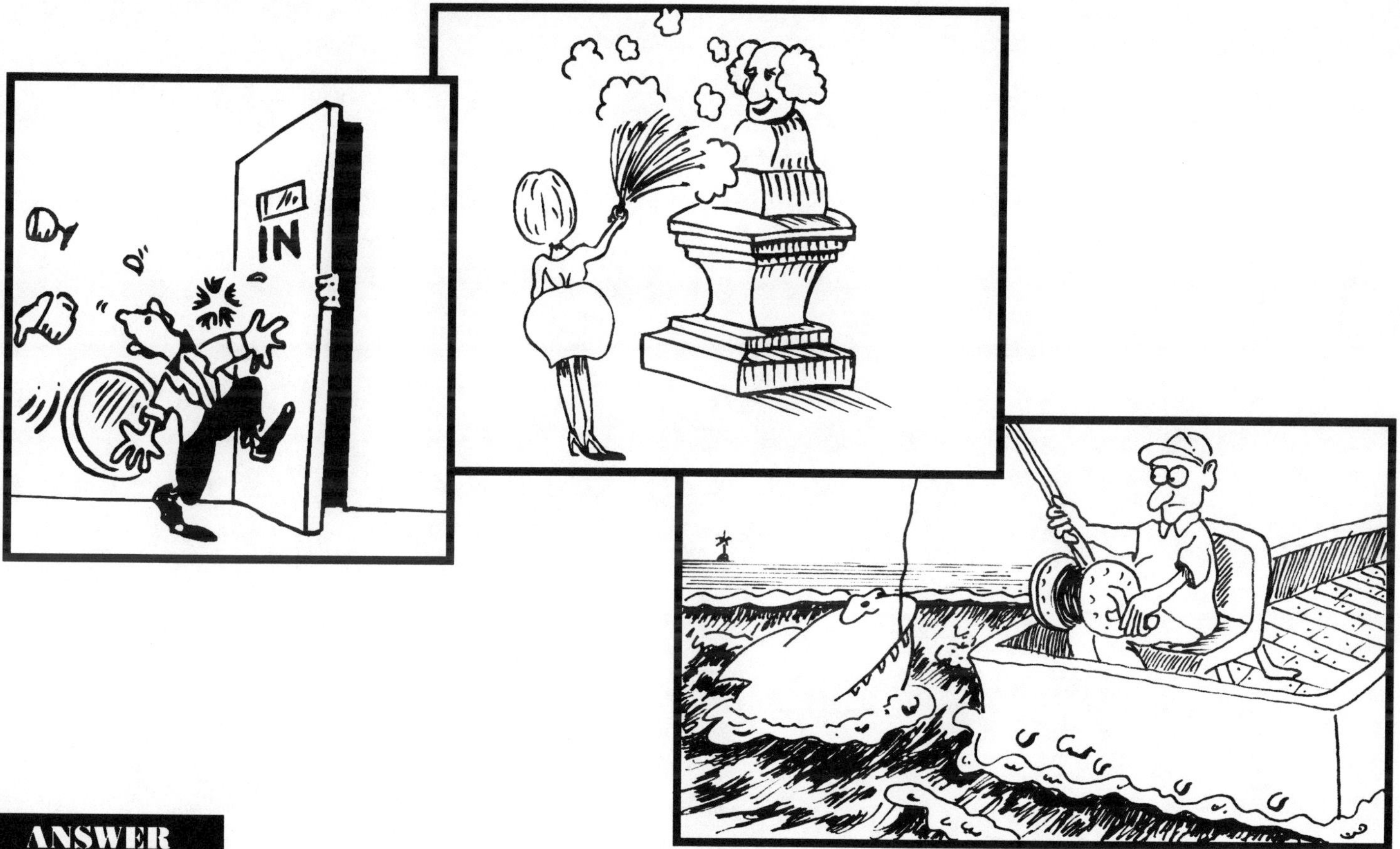
IN

ANSWER ON BACK

INDUSTRIAL

A "cheer" for Hollywood

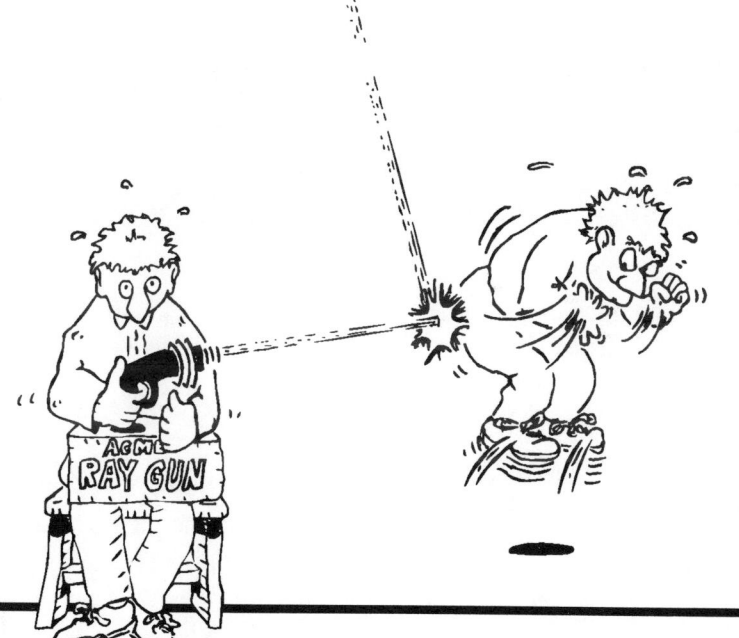

ACME
RAY GUN

ANSWER
ON BACK

42

HOORAY

What we don't want our competition to do

ANSWER ON BACK

SUCCEED

Produces perfect vision

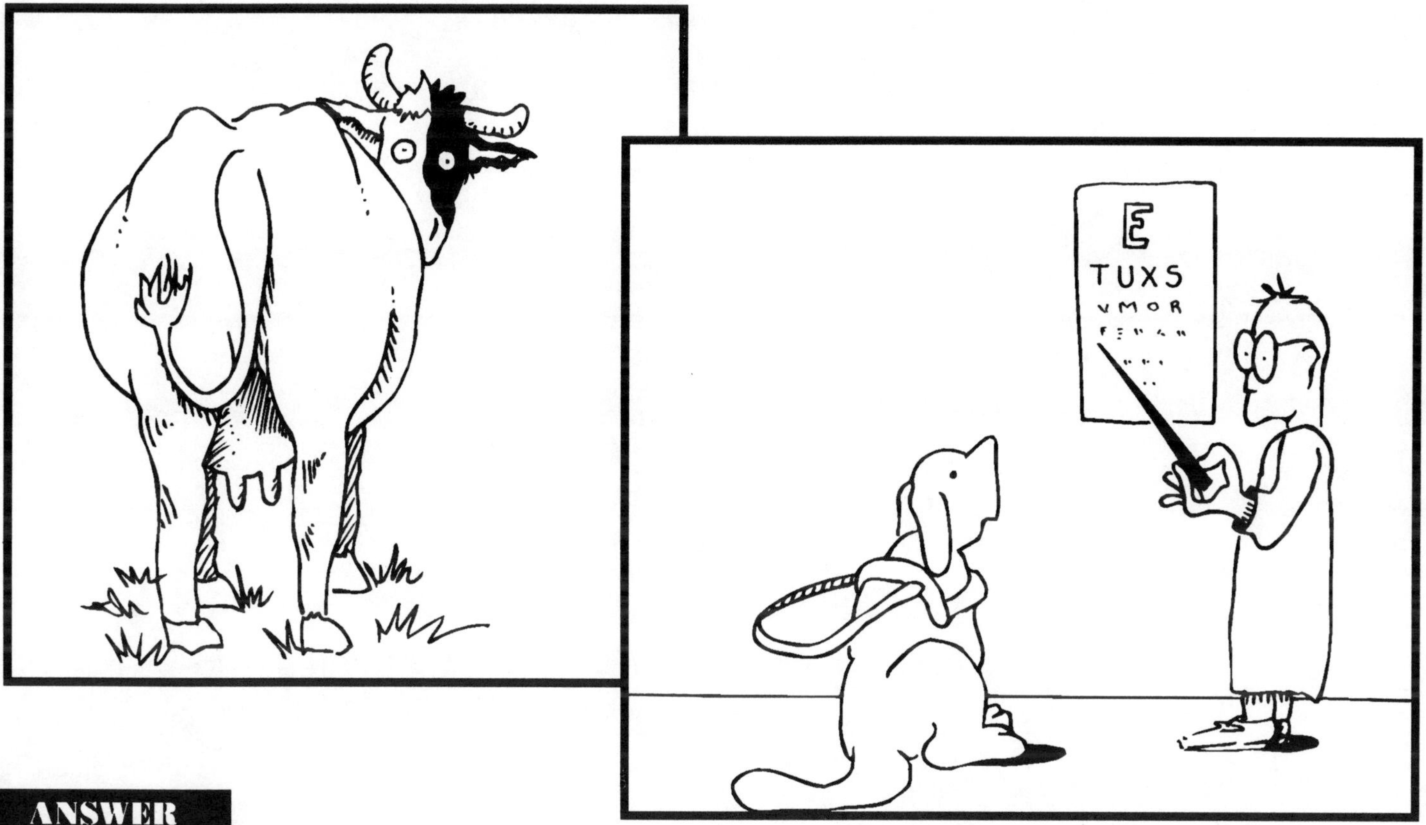
E
TUXS
VMOR

ANSWER ON BACK

HINDSIGHT

A shopping tool

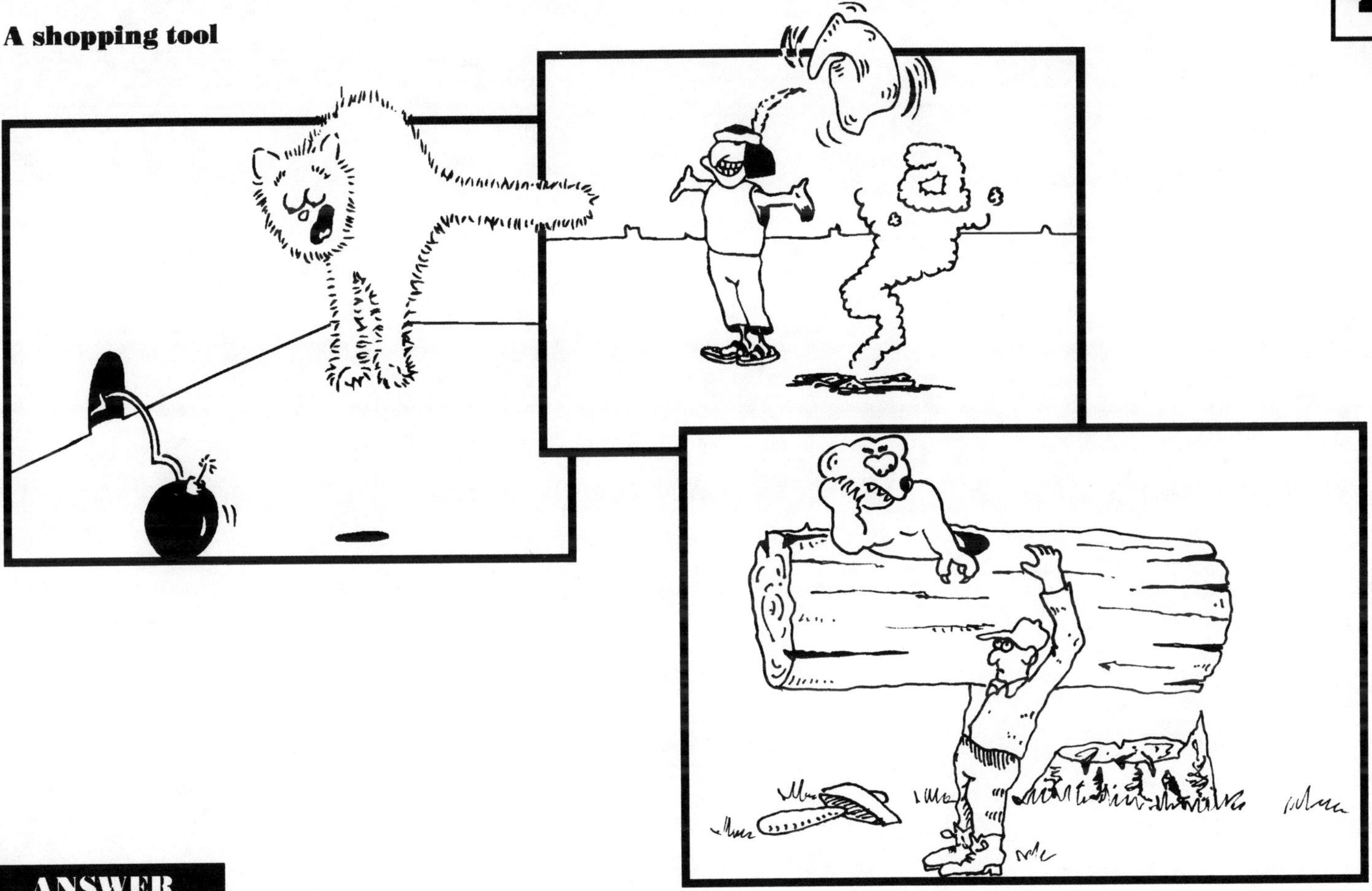
a

ANSWER ON BACK

CATALOG

Paul Gruen is a world class game inventor.
Among his 42 credits are such classics as
Payday™ and Bonkers™ and
the newly notorious
Splat™.